The Friendly Classroom for a Small Planet

A Handbook on Creative Approaches
to Living and Problem Solving for Children

by
—Priscilla Prutzman—Lee Stern—M. Leonard Burger—
—Gretchen Bodenhamer—

Illustrations by
—Dana McMurray —

Children's Creative Response to Conflict Program
Fellowship of Reconciliation

New Society Publishers

Philadelphia, PA

Gabriola Island, BC

Inquiries regarding requests to reprint all or part of *The Friendly Classroom for a Small Planet* should be addressed to:
New Society Publishers
P.O. Box 189
Gabriola Island, BC V0R 1X0, Canada

USA ISBN 0-86571-128-3 Hardcover
USA ISBN 0-86571-129-1 Paperback

Canadian ISBN 1-55092-044-8 Hardback
Canadian ISBN 1-55092-045-6 Paperback

Printed in the United States of America

Cover and text design by Barbara Hirshkowitz.
Illustrations by Dana McMurray.
Music engraved by Music Art Company, New York, NY.

Grateful acknowledgment is made for use of the following material.
"Prisoners learn that there are alternatives to violent behavior." By permission of the author and the Staten Island *Advance*.
"Children's growth toward cooperation: The teacher's role." By permission of the author.
"Building friendship in the classroom." By permission of Evelyn Weiss.

Children's Creative Response to Conflict is a nonprofit, tax-exempt program affiliated with the Fellowship of Reconciliation (FOR), an association of women and men who have joined together to explore the power of love and truth for resolving human conflict. The American FOR is affiliated with the International FOR with headquarters in Alkmaar, The Netherlands.

For information about workshops and other CCRC services contact:
Children's Creative Response to Conflict
PO Box 271
Nyack, NY 10960

To order directly from the publisher, add $3.00 to the price of the first copy, and $1.00 for each additional copy (plus GST in Canada). Send check or money order to:
New Society Publishers,
P.O. Box 189, Gabriola Island, BC V0R 1X0, Canada

Table of Contents

Creative Response—Meeting the Challenge of Violence

This chapter presents the philosophy of the CCRC program, the themes on which it focuses and the skills it seeks to develop. It includes an introduction to the themes of cooperation, communication, affirmation and conflict resolution.

An Idea Grows—The Roots of Violence

This chapter gives a brief historical background of the project. It covers getting to the roots of conflict, the importance of transferring skills to everyday life and building a sense of trust.

Preparing and Planning—Some Preliminary Considerations

This covers the importance of creating a cooperative environment, offering three approaches: workshops, integration into daily classroom activities, and integration of themes and activities into curriculum. It also suggests ways of diagnosing the needs of the class and hints for planning a workshop. A sample workshop plan is included.

Getting Started—The Role of Facilitator

This chapter presents briefly some facilitation techniques and concepts, including ways of beginning and ending sessions. Suggestions are given for working in small groups.

The Challenge of Integration—Moving beyond the Workshop Approach

This chapter gives examples of how teachers have integrated these techniques into their classrooms and curricula.

Let's Get Acquainted—Exercises That Help Remember Names

Name games are fun loosening-up activities that help to develop a sense of community. Several examples are given that can be used throughout the year.

Freeing Ourselves Up—Loosening-up Activities
These activities encourage children to laugh and interact with each other in a playful way. This relieves tension and helps to increase the energy in a group. Many of these games help to focus on what is happening.

Let's Build Community—Learning to Cooperate
These cooperation activities offer an alternative to competitive games and help to develop a positive classroom atmosphere. Included are group cooperation drawings, drama games and other projects to help children work together successfully toward a positive final goal.

Do You Hear Me?—Learning to Communicate
Effective communication skills are important for resolving conflicts creatively. This chapter includes positive ways of improving listening, observation and speaking skills.

We Are All Special—Affirmation of Ourselves and Others
Poor self-image is at the root of many conflicts. Affirmation activities encourage children to feel positive about themselves and others. This chapter includes exercises that can be used with large groups or individuals.

A Notebook All about Me—Creating a Treasured Possession
Did you ever want to record all the nice things about yourself? This chapter offers several examples of how to do this by means of affirmation sheets. These include drawings of what children like to do and what they are good at, and written pages that encourage self-awareness.

Let's Make an Instrument—An Affirming Activity for Everyone
This chapter gives examples of musical instruments that can be made out of simple, inexpensive materials.

Sometimes We Can All Win—Creative Conflict Resolution
Often we think of conflicts as having only win-lose solutions. These activities help children see that there are many alternative ways of resolving problems, and that often we can find a win-win solution. Roleplaying, puppetry and decision making are some of the many conflict resolution activities suggested.

But How Do We Resolve the Problem?—Some Conflict Scenarios
This chapter includes specific examples of conflicts that are common to children in school, at home and elsewhere: conflicts between children and children, teachers and children, parents and children, and conflicts between adults. These can be used as examples for creating your own scenarios, skits, puppet shows and roleplays, and for problem solving.

Doesn't Anybody Understand?
The Need to Share Feelings and Develop Trust
These activities help to develop a consciousness in a group that promotes affirmation and communication. When children share their feelings openly, creative conflict resolution occurs. This chapter includes the sharing circle, trust games and activities that help children analyze the roles they play and the effects of exclusion.

How Did It Work?—Let's Evaluate
Evaluation activities help children feel that they are part of a group. They are also helpful to the teacher or facilitator in planning subsequent sessions and meeting the needs of participants more directly.

Why Only in Classrooms?—Expanding Our Skills to Meet Wider Needs
This chapter relates how CCRC ideas have been adapted for younger children, high school students, emotionally disturbed children and prisoners.

Appendix

Preface to the Second Trade Edition

Response to the twelve printings in the five previous editions of *Friendly Classroom* has been gratifying. Enthusiastic comments continue to pour in from teachers around the world who have made it a part of their classroom adventure. The book or parts of it have been translated into several languages and teacher workshops based on it have been held in Europe and the Philippines. In the United States, Children's Creative Response to Conflict (CCRC) has become an ongoing program in an increasing number of schools. Several graduate theses here and abroad have centered on the CCRC program. An important part of the book's success is due to every exercise and activity having been thoroughly tested over the years and modified or discarded in response to children's needs.

However, even while our ideas have evolved and broadened, our basic philosophy and perspective have remained the same as when FRIENDLY CLASSROOM was first published in 1974 as a "Preliminary Handbook" for teachers, by CCRC's predecessor, the Quaker Project on Community Conflict (QPCC). The following quotation from the preface to the first edition sums up our philosophy succinctly:

> During years of involvement in nonviolence training in all kinds of crises and potentially violent situations, the staff of the Quaker Project on Community Conflict (QPCC) has become increasingly aware that the seeds of conflict become instilled at a very early age in the patterns of hostile or violent response to human situations learned by young children from adults, older children or their peers. We have also become aware that teachers and educators have not been prepared with tools and methods appropriate for changing these patterns.
>
> Believing that the wider conflicts in our society and the world will continue to threaten our civilization until we learn to deal with our personal and community problems constructively and creatively, in 1972 QPCC set about tailoring the tools, skills and methods it had developed so they could be adapted to children at the grade school level, before negative responses become ingrained. Our hope is to revolutionize their responses to conflict situations by actually involving them in working out creative new approaches.
>
> The present workshops cover a broader scope than conflict resolution. It soon became apparent that to develop creative responses to conflict, children (and adults, too) need to begin to understand both their own feelings and the feelings of others. They need to become aware of the advantages of working together, rather than against one another, to solve problems. Cooperation and community-building exercises therefore occupy a significant part of the handbook, and almost always precede exercises in conflict resolution. They are part of our effort to provide a suitable, humane, "life-support system" for children in our schools.

Our particular program has three main goals in the classroom: (1) to promote growth toward a community in which children are capable and desirous of open communication; (2) to help children gain insights into the nature of human feelings and share their own feelings; and (3) to explore with children the unique personal ways in which they can respond to problems and begin to prevent or solve conflicts.

As trainers, we know it requires the greatest humility to become involved in a child's life. Conflict resolution requires a great deal of careful reflection, as negative overtones often develop where violence is suppressed. Indeed, some aggression and anger are desirable. The aim in working on conflict is not to abolish it, but to enable children to deal with it creatively over a period of time and to direct it into constructive channels.

As interest in this field has grown, a number of books have appeared which use some of the ideas and concepts presented here, and likewise various curricula have been developed on the basis of our work. We have resisted pressures to turn the CCRC program into a standardized curriculum. The reason for this may be gleaned from chapter three, "Preparing and Planning," which discusses the importance of adapting the material to the needs and circumstances of each particular class or group of children. We realize that this requires the teacher's careful observation and assessment of classroom dynamics and needs. We are also aware of the many demands and restrictions the teacher already faces which limit options and usurp energy. But when the needs of the children are addressed, the teacher will find a new sense of community in the classroom that lightens the atmosphere, facilitates the teaching of cognitive skills and introduces a new spirit of fun and adventure.

Teachers who are excited by the techniques and philosophy presented here will want to subscribe to CCRC's newsletter, *Sharing Space,* which supplements this book. We hope they will also share their insights, ideas and classroom experiences with others through its pages. This is, after all, an extension of the idea of sharing inherent in the CCRC program. Another CCRC resource is the new book, *Children's Songs for a Friendly Planet,* published jointly with Educators for Social Responsibility and the Riverside Disarmament Program. The CCRC program is also preparing graded activity books for publication as this edition goes to press. Readers are invited to write to CCRC for further information. (See p. 119 for a full description of CCRC services and p. 127 for the CCRC branch closest to you.)

Acknowledgements

It has been exciting to work on this edition with New Society Publishers. They have been more than helpful in working out all of the arrangements and details. It is also gratifying that we now share the publisher of *A Manual on Nonviolence and Children,* produced by our sister program in Philadelphia, the Committee on Nonviolence and Children. We have both benefitted immeasurably from our sharing over the past sixteen years.

We are grateful to the many friends who contributed their skills to this book. Kay Reynolds gave generously of her time and editorial skills. Jude Johnson spent untold hours on the painstaking task of revising the bibliography and index. Grants from the Trustees of the New York Yearly Meeting of Friends and from the Institute for World Order (now the World Policy Institute) made possible the publication of earlier editions. The Fellowship of Reconciliation, with which CCRC is affiliated, has been generous with office space, services and support.

We want to acknowledge people who have worked with similar groups or who have inspired, lauded, nurtured and funded those of us involved in creative conflict resolution for children. There are too many to mention here, but we want especially to acknowledge the support of Cathy and Jim McGinnis, Kathleen Kanet, Fran Schmidt, Betty Reardon, Elise Boulding, Jeff Brown, Barry Childers, John Donaghy, Lillian Genser, Helen Hafner, Althea Postlethwaite, Patricia Mische, Bill Harley, William Kreidler, Evelyn Weiss, Sarah Pirtle, Ruth Pelham, Jamie Walker, Pat Paatfoort, Anita St. Claire, Larry Swift, Kathy Bickmore, Tom Roderick, Shelly Berman, Linda Lantieri, Ellen Raider, Lyn Fine, and the teachers in the District 15 Peace Education program and P.S. 75, in New York City. Phillip Strell, Luis Mercado, Sylvia Oberferst, Esther Rosenfeld, Roberta Kirshbaum and Anthony Alvarado are among the school administrators who have supported CCRC's work over the years. Without the help of Ruth Imbesi, Lawrence Apsey, Marge Rice and Sue Hadley, CCRC could not have moved forward so dramatically. Nor without the dedicated assistance of CCRC's current and past staff in Nyack, which includes in addition to the authors Edna Adler, Petra Bertram, Kelly Cannard, Sarah Daykin, Suzanne Goodemote, John Vidoli, Mary Sarsheen, Joyce Davison, Jane Ann Smith, Liz Halsey Sproul, Colombe Hearth, Marianne MacQueen, Joe Smith, Moriah Vecchia, Craig Wachsman, David Zarembka, Larry Frommer, Fred Evans, Lauren Stern, Mae Sakharov, Loren Weybright, Beate Roggenbuck, Ed Hayes, Connie Jump, Kit Hastings, Judy Lightstone, Nancy, Doug, Kenda and Devin Helfrich, Paula Conner, Rose Marie Ortenberg, Sally McAfee, Lawrence Wofford, Lisel Lowen, Judy Garson, Terry Murray, James Williams, Lynn King, Emma Gonzalez, and Diane Goodman.

Priscilla Prutzman and Lee Stern
February 1988

How to Use This Book

It is the authors' hope that this book will be used as a guide for creative experimentation in the classroom. Teachers will recognize how an affirming, cooperative atmosphere in a friendly classroom can significantly reduce tensions and discipline problems, especially when combined with games and exercises that are both fun and valuable affective education techniques. Such a class atmosphere can enhance both the children's abilities to learn and the teacher's ability for effective and creative teaching. However, this is a *process* which takes time, patience and careful planning. The reward will be each small response in which a child—often quite unexpectedly—indicates that he or she has not only understood these ideas but is actually making them a part of his or her inner resources.

A word about the organization of this book. Chapters six through sixteen form what formerly was called the "Tool and Technique Guide." Here will be found the specific games, exercises and other tools which are the heart of the Children's Creative Response to Conflict program. Although given here in a natural sequence with each chapter constituting a theme or part of a theme, there is much overlapping of themes in these techniques, and they may be used in quite different orders.

We hope that you will find the appendix a rich source of materials for use in your classroom and for further personal development of CCRC ideas as well as related ones.

In using this book with your group, you will probably find new variations and additions of your own. Many of these may come from children themselves. The authors lay no claim to originality of the ideas presented here. They come from many sources. The creative response approach belongs to all who use it. Please share your new insights with us so that we may incorporate them into our newsletter thus helping to enrich the experience of others.

Careful study of the planning chapters (three, four and five) should make implementation of the tools and techniques far more effective and successful.

Foreword

Albert Einstein once said that with the advent of the nuclear age, everything has changed but the human race's way of thinking. In this statement he pointed out the necessity of thinking about conflict in new and less destructive ways. Conflict takes many forms. Whether global disputes between superpowers, strategic differences between businesspeople or arguments between schoolchildren, they can take either a constructive or destructive course. They can lead to lively controversy or deadly quarrel depending upon how they are managed.

There is much conflict in our schools—conflict that too frequently takes a destructive course. Many students never develop the attitudes and skills to handle productively the conflicts they face in the course of their lives. Much of their knowledge of handling conflict is acquired haphazardly and in contexts (television, video and movies) which emphasize destructive methods. If students were systematically taught how to manage conflicts constructively, they would become less vulnerable to emotional disorders, suicide, violence and other forms of antisocial behavior. Beyond this, we must prepare our students to deal constructively with the conflicts that inevitably occur among nations in our nuclear age.

The Friendly Classroom for a Small Planet is an excellent tool for teachers who wish to create a classroom environment enabling students to develop a sense of self-worth, build community and acquire the skills of creative conflict resolution. This book wisely stresses the importance of incorporating the processes of cooperation and conflict resolution into the day-to-day activities of the classroom. It is not enough to teach the concepts of creative conflict resolution; the child's classroom experience must exemplify the ideas taught. In addition to providing a valuable orientation, this book offers many useful techniques, games and activities to establish the necessary context for children to cope with conflict. Any educator wishing to help children learn to solve problems creatively will be rewarded by turning to this book.

Morton Deutsch
Teachers College
Columbia University

1 Creative Response
Meeting the Challenge of Violence

Violence in our society is pervasive. In the schools, where tension builds up and conflicts go unresolved, assaults on children, teachers and property are commonplace. Educational institutions which should provide a positive environment for resisting the drift toward violence are seldom effective in dealing with the causes of antisocial behavior. They often retreat to measures of security or take hostile actions against the offenders.

Yet the very attempt to stamp out violence by methods which are themselves violent towards children in conflict only confirms the notion that violence is an acceptable, if not preferable, method of solving problems. Such methods are dehumanizing and fail to provide children with positive alternatives to violent patterns of behavior. Our experience shows that children—especially young children—will learn far more from the ways we respond to aggression and conflict than they will learn from our words. We see the teaching of moral behavior primarily as a matter of how we *act* rather than of what we say. What we say is important, but even more important is that it corresponds to what we do.

The basic philosophy of the Children's Creative Response to Conflict program is to create an atmosphere among children and adults which is warm, affirming and supportive. Only in such an atmosphere is it possible for children to learn how to deal with each other and with conflict in a humane and constructive manner.

2 An Idea Grows
The Roots of Violence

Getting to the Roots

In its approach to conflict resolution, the Children's Creative Response to Conflict (CCRC) program seeks to deal with the roots of conflict and not merely the symptoms. The goal is to encourage teachers and others who work with children to move beyond the treatment of isolated crisis situations by developing a positive dynamic which motivates children to respond to conflict constructively. Focusing exclusively on the immediate crisis—whether it is in the classroom, the community or between nations—is like cutting off a weed at the soil line, while underground the hidden roots continue to send up new and vigorous shoots. The roots of conflict lie deep in our culture and are reflected in the kinds of behavior our society promotes: competition, hostility in response to aggression or fear, and the putdowns we hear daily in the classrooms, corridors and playgrounds of our schools.

We find that children develop positive self-concepts and learn to be open, sharing and cooperative much more effectively when they become part of a community in which these attributes are the norm. In such an atmosphere they discover better ways to relate to one another as well as to themselves. It is not enough to talk about these ideas; to be effective they must be reflected in the organization of the classroom. Compare for example a circle seating arrangement to a traditional classroom structure: how much more eloquent the circle is as an expression of equality. Instead of simply telling children that violence is wrong or evil, we teach this by building a positive classroom environment where violence seems totally out of place and our actions are examples of constructive approaches to problem solving.

We present children with tools—enjoyable tools—that encourage them to discover for themselves solutions to problems and conflicts arising out of their own real-life experiences. It is *they* who decide which of these will be most helpful to them in terms of their own personal goals. And what fertile imaginations they have! What amazingly creative solutions they sometimes come up with! This process—of encouraging children to actively participate in the resolution of conflicts—is the CCRC philosophy in action. And the best way to understand the theory behind the process is to practice it!

Some may conclude that the CCRC program shelters children and renders them incapable of dealing with the real world. But our experience demonstrates the contrary. When children are provided with a loving, supportive environment, they are better able to meet whatever conflict may arise, inside or outside the classroom, in a creative and conciliatory manner.

We are not opposed to all conflict. Sometimes our most significant growth comes through conflict, especially when we learn to deal with it constructively. But many conflicts are unnecessary, wasteful and serve no purpose. This type of conflict often disappears when we deal effectively with the roots.

Thus parents tell us of how children who participate in CCRC workshops change their behavior toward siblings from belligerence to consideration. And a participant in our course for teachers feels that CCRC's presence in the public school where she teaches has contributed to the decrease in fights. When fights still do occur, she notices that students attempt to stop them instead of either standing around and watching, or even encouraging them.

Skills Are Not Enough

The carryover of positive attitudes and skills from the classroom into real-life situations was not apparent in our earliest work with children. Because we did not fully sense the depth or complexity of our task—how to nurture in children the seeds of compassion rather than violence—we attempted to teach conflict resolution skills without proper concern for a supportive classroom atmosphere. Though we had experience working with adults developing new patterns of thought and action, we came to understand through our work in the classroom that children learn most effectively through experience. Thus the environment is of paramount importance. We also came to understand that the teacher has a key role in the creation of the proper environment. The following account by one of our facilitators illustrates one way we learned this.

> Since the beginning of the year we had done only conflict resolution exercises with the classes. At first observation these seemed to go very well. Then we presented a skit to a second grade class, using puppets to portray a conflict involving an older sister and a younger brother. The skit opened with the puppet portraying the younger brother on stage holding a book. The puppet portraying the older sister arrived on stage looking for her book. The conflict ensued as the sister demanded the book and the brother refused to give it up. At this point we interrupted the puppet show and directed the children to form small groups and come up with solutions to the problem. The children with their adult facilitators came up with solutions and then presented them to the entire class in skits using puppets. The solutions were heartwarming: the sister reading the book to her brother, taking her brother into her room to help him choose a more appropriate book, taking the brother to the library to let him pick out his own books. We were delighted with these solutions. However, one of the teachers asked us a provocative question: "Do you think the children really believe the solutions they come up with?" When we asked the

teacher what she meant, she said that children—even very young children—learn quickly the kinds of answers that teachers like to hear and therefore provide teachers with such answers.

We held one-to-one conferences with all the children in the class and discovered that the teacher's perceptions were in many cases correct. Using a different conflict, we asked the children what they would do in the situation. Some children parroted back almost word-for-word what they had been taught, indicating no true assimilation of the substance of the lesson, while others answered "I'd punch him in the nose" or "I'd go into his room and take something of his."

Building a Sense of Trust

To us it seemed a re-evaluation was in order. We realized that in order for conflict resolution techniques to become concrete for the children, they needed to be in an environment where cooperation and trust prevailed. Thus we set about creating such a supportive atmosphere. During the last half of 1973–74, we developed and tested many exercises using the themes of *cooperation, affirmation* and *communication*. Through this process, we were able to build a sense of community and a feeling of trust among the children we worked with. We could then realistically hope that the children would understand and accept these techniques into their own lives.

This example reflects the experimental nature of our approach. Many changes have occurred in the CCRC program since its inception in 1972. It has been a period of learning and growth. We have learned from the teachers with whom we have worked as well as from the writing and experience of many other groups working to develop creative interpersonal relations. But most of all, we have learned from the children.

3 Preparing and Planning
Some Preliminary Considerations

Creating a Cooperative Environment

The thematic arrangement of the remaining chapters reflects their relationship to a common goal. That goal is the creation of an environment which enables children to build a sense of community, know their worth as individuals and develop the skills of creative conflict resolution. Each aspect of this environment relates to and builds on the others. A relaxed and comfortable environment is necessary for people to experience cooperation and community. A sense of comunity promotes feelings of belonging and enhances children's concept of themselves and others. And a positive self-concept enables children to improve communication skills which are essential to creative conflict resolution. Each chapter of this handbook focuses on one aspect of this environment and contributes to its creation. In this environment, children are able to internalize these concepts of creative conflict resolution and act from them in situations that arise throughout their lives.

Acquiring the skills of creative conflict resolution is an ongoing process, and occasional setbacks are to be expected. To be used successfully, these skills require practical experience. Further, no attempt has been made to catalogue all the insights that can be derived from the techniques described here. There are many new insights that you will find. The main point is to look for the activities that your group needs.

These techniques require your constant evaluation. Do not regard them as solutions to problems. Some problems may be unsolvable. But these techniques help the teacher to build a more positive atmosphere in the class and solve those conflicts which children are willing to solve. Equally as important as voluntary participation is the need for children to want to solve conflicts. Interest in finding creative solutions grows as the advantages are observed. With time, creative problem solving becomes a natural response.

Three Formats

There are three formats you can use to introduce the themes and techniques of creative conflict resolution into the classroom. The first is the *workshop* format, which is a distinct and separate activity in the class. A workshop is planned out beforehand in detail and may not relate to curriculum or other aspects of the class. A workshop may include several loosening-up exercises, the main goal being to have fun and build a sense of community. This format is described in more detail in **Planning a Workshop,** page 7.

The second format is *integration into the daily activities of the class.* In this format, the themes of creative conflict resolution are incorporated into ongoing activities and can occur at regular intervals throughout the day, week and year. For instance, when children arrive in the morning, ask them what good thing happened on the way to school. Or when they are going on vacation, ask what they would like to do on vacation. An example of this second format is discussed in chapter five.

The third format is *integration into the curriculum.* One example is to plan a writing assignment whose goal is personal affirmation, or a science experiment whose goal is cooperation. An example of this approach is given in chapter five.

Our experience with the workshop model has shown that it provides a good introduction to the goals and methods of creative conflict resolution. We hope that teachers who begin with this approach are challenged to integrate these themes into other activities and the curriculum so that a supportive atmosphere is built into the total classroom experience rather than provided only during the workshop period.

Teachers familiar with related forms of group process may develop confidence quickly in integrating these techniques into their class activities and curricula. For others it is helpful to realize that most of these techniques are experiential. Without some previous exposure to similar activities, it is often difficult to grasp the full significance of the exercises and carry them out effectively. Teachers might want to get together to try out techniques or discuss plans. The remainder of this chapter is designed to give suggestions for planning and facilitating goals and activities for your own class.

Diagnosing the Needs of the Class

Although you may know a great deal about individual children in the class, the first step in planning a workshop is to gather information about how children behave as a class. One way to do this is to keep a log of what happens in the classroom over a period of several days with the following questions in mind:

–How do you feel about the children?
–How do the children feel about you?
–How well do the children know each other and you?
–Do the children like each other?

–Do the children have fun?

–Do you have fun?

–Do any activities happen spontaneously?

–How much freedom do the children have?

–Are there emotionally disturbed children?

–Are the children ranked?

–Are there age differences in the classroom?

–Do the children participate in the creation of any activities?

–Who has the most power?

–Do children put each other down?

–Are there personality problems?

–Are there cliques?

–Do the children fight back?

–How do children behave behind your back?

–Do the children behave differently in your absence?

–How do the children react to substitute teachers?

–How do children react to visitors?

–What is the level of parent involvement?

–What is the atmosphere of the school?

–Is the atmosphere of the school different from that of your classroom?

–How do the students feel about the administration?

–Is there a punishment system?

The answers to these questions should give you an overall view of what is going on in your class and clarify how the main CCRC themes relate to your group. You might ask yourself questions that deal directly with these themes:

–Is there a cooperative mood in the class?

–Do the children feel good about themselves and others?

–Do the children listen to each other?

–Do the children communicate clearly?

–How are conflicts resolved?

If a sense of community is lacking, you can start with cooperation games. Personal affirmation may become an important goal if children have a low level of confidence. If communication is a problem, you can work on listening, observing and speaking skills. If children are positive, cooperative and communicate easily, you can begin working on conflict resolution skills.

Planning a Workshop

In planning, consider the goal of the workshop. What do you hope to accomplish with the session? There may be a single goal: to introduce an idea, define conflict, build cooperation, develop communication skills, or solve a particular problem in the classroom. Or there may be more than one goal: to familiarize children with a specific technique such as roleplaying or puppetry, and to work on cooperation and conflict resolution. The goal may also revolve around a specific theme such as finding creative solutions to problems children face daily.

The next step is finding activities which match your goals. We recommend you review all activities described in this book before selecting ones for your class. It is helpful to plan with someone else in the group such as a student, a student aide, a parent, or a student teacher. One way to get ideas for the plan is to brainstorm possible activities (see chapter thirteen, page 63). Think about possible activities with the following questions in mind:

–Are the activities all related to the main goal?

–Is there a progression from easier to more difficult exercises?

–Are the activities related to each other and ordered so that there is an obvious flow to the session?

–Is there enough change of pace, alternating talking with doing?

–Is there a mix of large and small group activities?

–Are there opportunities for everyone to speak, or is there a possibility that a few might dominate?

–Do children have the opportunity to move around?

–Does the structure allow children to offer input?

–Will participants have fun?

–Are these exercises that everyone will participate in?

–Is there a time for evaluation to occur?

Elements in a Plan

In addition to choosing appropriate goals and activities, in planning a workshop you need to consider how to begin and end a session. Do you want to begin with a warm-up exercise, and if so, which one? If you plan a series of workshops, you may want to begin each one in a similar way, with a game or a ritual of holding hands in a circle. Most teachers have a good idea of what works with their own class. In general, if a class is bored easily or has difficulty working as a group, an exciting group-building activity is important. If a class does not respond well to a ritual, vary the introductory exercises according to the goal or theme of the workshop. Activities such as singing or light-and-livelies add energy and create a more relaxed atmosphere. Choose activities appropriate for the size of the group.

An Example of Planning

The following is an example of how to choose goals and plan a workshop for a class. It is early in the school year. Children are not cooperating with each other and seem to be isolated. Most children do not know each other's names, and a sense of community is absent. You think that cliques are developing, especially among the boys and the girls. The children are the same age, although their reading and writing levels vary. Based on these observations you come up with the following goals: to relax the group, to help people learn each other's names, to develop a sense of community.

You think about the various activities described in this book which relate to the goals of introduction. They include the *Name Game Song, Introducing through a Puppet, Memory Name Game,* and *Introductory Name Game.*

You don't like to sing, so you eliminate the *Name Game Song.* You're afraid the children will find puppets babyish, so you discard *Introducing Through a Puppet.* Since you want people to learn each other's names well, you decide that the *Memory Name Game* is the best exercise to open with.

You also want to do some loosening-up activities to relax the group. You consider pantomime games such as *Herman-Hermina* and *Pantomime This Object* as well as light-and-livelies including *Zoom* and *Elephant and Palm Tree.* Since people will have been sitting for a very long time, you choose *Elephant and Palm Tree* because it involves everyone standing up in a circle and being fairly active. Also, there is an element of cooperation in this exercise which relates to your goal of building community.

You want one more exciting game to be sure the group is relaxed and having fun. You still like the idea of doing pantomime, so you choose *Herman-Hermina.* This has everyone sitting in a circle again. To emphasize the idea of cooperation you think about longer cooperation activities such as *Tinker Toys, Group Drawing, Grab Bag Dramatics, Machine Building* and *Monster Making. Machine Building* and *Monster Making* assure the most cooperation and of the two, you feel that *Monster Making* is less threatening since the worse the drawing, the better the monster. So you choose *Monster Making.* Since it is a fairly long activity, all you need is a closing or an evaluation. Your final plan looks like this:

1. *Memory Name Game*
2. *Elephant and Palm Tree*
3. *Herman-Hermina*
4. *Monster Making*
5. *Evaluation*

You are not sure how to do the evaluation so you choose a very simple format. You will ask children to name one thing they liked about the session and one thing they would like to see changed.

You would like a good closing for the workshop but you are not sure that the mood will be right. So you leave open the possibility of a closing circle in which you will ask children to name one thing they like about the monsters. You can decide if a closing circle is appropriate after the evaluation.

Flexibility in Your Plans

Any plan should be flexible. The plan is a means to an end, not an end in itself. Change the plan to accommodate the needs of the class. Providing this flexibility shows the class that the workshop is uniquely for them rather than a standardized procedure into which they must fit. When people have a say in what happens, participation increases and a supportive atmosphere results. You can make changes in the plan either at the beginning or as the workshop develops.

For further notes on amending your plans, see **Agenda Setting,** page 12.

4 Getting Started
The Role of Facilitator

Much has been written about facilitation; we mention here only a few points that may prove helpful.

An important task of the facilitator is to keep things moving. Sometimes it is more valuable to continue a good discussion than to move on to the next activity. It is the facilitator's job to ask the group whether it prefers to keep to the agenda or extend the current activity. Often the facilitator clarifies and summarizes opinions to relate the discussions to the goal of the workshop. The facilitator also checks periodically to see if the session is moving in a way agreeable to the group.

Another important function of the facilitator is to ensure that everyone's point of view is heard, and looking at differences becomes a positive learning experience rather than contending to prove who is right. The facilitator provides an example by showing warm concern and interest for the participants, affirming them and their contributions. It is the facilitator's responsibility to maintain the cohesiveness of the group.

It is important for the facilitator to balance the needs of individuals with the goals of the group. People should feel comfortable contributing to the group. There should be an equal distribution of power, and a feeling that everyone has a say in what happens. People should have equal time to talk, and it is the facilitator's responsibility to encourage those reticent to speak and discourage those who monopolize the discussion. Each member of the group should feel accepted by the others.

A **circle structure** is an important way of showing that everyone participates equally and no one is more or less important than anyone else.

There are two simple **ground rules** which apply to every activity:
(1) Everyone has a chance to participate; and
(2) Everyone respects the contributions of others.

Voluntary participation in activities is equally important. If an activity is affirming and fun, everyone will want to participate. If some do not want to participate, provide an activity that they can do quietly in another part of the room. Just as they can choose to leave, they can also choose to return. Similarly, allow children to "pass" at any time during an activity.

Some Special Techniques

Here are some ideas for beginning and ending your sessions.

Agenda setting at the beginning of an activity is a process for sharing the goals and plan with the group, and getting consensus to proceed. If anyone does not understand the planned activities, now is the time to explain them. For example, "*Monster Making* is a cooperative drawing exercise where we all draw parts of a monster and put them together." After going over the plan, ask children if they are comfortable going ahead with it. A group will accept a plan that takes their needs into account. If there is general disagreement with the plan, it is the facilitator's role to help the group come up with a new one quickly so that the entire time is not spent deciding what to do.

Use **quiet time** to settle a group which is noisy or anxious. Ask children to listen to the sounds in the room and focus their thoughts for the session. Quiet time is personally affirming as well as group building.

Evaluation encourages student participation in the form of feedback at the end of an activity. Use evaluations often and follow up suggestions as quickly as possible. Evaluations are helpful in planning subsequent sessions since they needs of participants more directly. (Please see chapter sixteen on evaluation.) In addition to encouraging feedback, be sure to continue evaluating the group and your own role so that you choose nonthreatening activities that will be positive experiences. Your skill in matching goals and activities will increase as you go along.

It is important to bring each activity to a definite **closing**. One way is to have an evaluation. Another way is to end with a song that children particularly enjoy. Sometimes a special mood develops during an activity which is characterized by an exciting feeling of togetherness or personal sharing. A **closing circle** is a good way to end this kind of session. People may link arms or hold hands while they respond to a specific question, such as "What is one word that describes how you are feeling right now?" or "Could you say something you like about the person next to you?" Use this method only when people are feeling positive about themselves and others, and responses to the questions can be genuine.

A **quiet time** may also close the session. Like the closing circle, this has to be spontaneous. It requires a certain mood to be effective. A quiet time in which children think about what the group has been doing can be a joyful experience.

While many things influence how a group works together, the techniques described here contribute to an affirmative and cooperative atmosphere in which put downs and other forms of violence decline.

Small Groups

Another job of the facilitator is to decide when to use small groups. For certain kinds of activities a small group (six to eight people) is more appropriate than a large one. You can use small groups any time a discussion is to occur. The small group allows greater participation by people who are reticent in a large group but feel free to open up in a small one. As in any group, allow equal opportunity for everyone to speak, and praise or acknowledge but never ridicule any contribution.

There are many ways to divide the class into small groups: use preplanned groups, count off by numbers or apples-pears-bananas-oranges, or allow children to choose groups on their own. While the latter involves the most free choice, take care to avoid the development of cliques. Drawing numbers of out a hat is time consuming but allows the teacher to control the size of groups. Simply assigning children to groups is fast but does not allow any student input. The more choices children have, the more they will participate in the activity. Choose a method that works with your group, and stick to it as much as possible. This will lend a regularity to the process and contribute to the success of each small group activity.

Some teachers may hesitate to divide a class into small groups because they cannot imagine the small groups being able to work on their own. One possibility is to let small groups choose their own facilitators, and review the planned activity with them. Student teachers, teacher aides, parents, and community volunteers can be used as small group facilitators in the beginning of the year. Later, after several weeks or months of small group activities, experiment without adult facilitators. Be sure that the facilitators review the ground rules (everyone gets a chance to participate and everyone respects the contributions of others.)

Once you have established small groups, be sure the goals and process of the activity are clear to everyone. Also, it is important to identify the facilitator in each group. The facilitators should encourage participants to form circles and start with an attention-grabbing question. Often called a "whip" or a "snap" question, its purpose is to focus the group's attention and establish an atmosphere of mutual affirmation and participation. A good "whip" question is interesting and personal but not difficult. For instance, "What is a good movie you have seen lately?" The question might also be related to the small group activity. In a small group *Storytelling,* some appropriate questions are: "What's your favorite kind of story? Do you have a story you especially like? What would you like our story to be about? If you were going to start a story, what would the first line be?" Keep answers brief so that everyone gets a chance to respond to each question. The facilitator may even use these answers to begin a story.

The facilitator in the small group *Storytelling* also determines who speaks and for how long. After the *Storytelling* , ask the following questions: "What is one thing you liked about the story? Did you feel that your part of the story was listened to? How do you think we should share the main ideas of our story with the rest of the class?" Decide who will report to the class and what they will say. Sharing what happened in small groups builds community in the class as well as cooperation in the small group.

If someone is put down, the facilitator should affirm that child along with anyone else troubled by the event and deal with the offender later. The facilitator's good feelings about the group will carry over to the children. But if problems cannot be handled by simple affirmations, do not sacrifice the group for one individual. Children who do not want to participate should not be forced. Instead, encourage them to join later; they will join when they feel ready. Children who decide not to participate should do something on their own and not disturb the rest of the group.

The small group facilitator should be aware of the whole class. If one group doesn't want to do what the rest of the class is doing, that group should ask the others' approval to do something else. If approval is denied, the small group should return to the original plan. Otherwise it will not seem fair to other groups and the sense of community will decline. If one group finishes the planned activity early, someone from that group should find out how much time others need to finish. If necessary, groups should negotiate any changes in the schedule. If others need more time, groups finishing early can disscuss what they did.

5 The Challenge of Integration
Moving beyond the Workshop Approach

Integrating Techniques into the Classroom

There are many ways to make creative response to conflict a part of the classroom. One is to have a daily sharing circle whose discussion topic is determined by the children. This can be a time for everyone to discuss problems in the class or for each person to share positive things about him/herself. Another possibility is to use loosening-up activities to release tension wherever anxiety in the classrom is high. Use affirmation techniques such as *Affirmation Valentines, Stocking Fillers* and *Silhouettes* to encourage positive feelings throughout the year. Or set aside a special time in the morning, after lunch or just before dismissal for everyone to gather and have fun. This approach can be more spontaneous than the workshop format, although you may want to do some planning early in the year.

One teacher shared with us how he integrated *Conflict Story Reading* into his fourth grade classroom and sustained the students' interest over a three-day period. It surprised the teacher that such a discussion could take place, especially since many of the children themselves fought frequently. The first day he outlined the main conflict in Ezra Jack Keats' *Goggles,* in which some older boys try to steal a pair of goggles from two younger ones. Without giving away the ending, he asked the children to brainstorm possible solutions and to everyone's amazement filled the blackboard with over forty ideas. Children copied down all the possible solutions in their notebooks and then discussed which solutions seemed absurd or unusable and why. The next day the teacher brought in the book and read the whole story to the class. The discussion of solutions resumed. For homework the teacher asked his students to choose the three most realistic solutions to the conflict. On the third day, children discussed their choices. The teacher asked children to distinguish solutions involving or leading to violence from those that did not. The length and seriousness of the ensuing discussion of possible outcomes surprised the teacher.

Integration into the Curriculum

In integrating creative responses into the curriculum you are limited only by your imagination. Several affirmation exercises relate directly to reading and writing skills, such as *If My Feet Could Talk, An Interview with a Friend,* and the *Affirmation Notebook* pages.

The following example shows how one teacher integrated the themes of creative response into her fourth grade reading curriculum. The teacher wanted to prepare her children for a reading test in a way that was affirming and cooperative yet fun for her students. She chose to do *Picture Games* (see page 47) over a three-week period. The first week she had the class create a set of games combining pictures and words from the vocabulary list. Each game consisted of a picture with a series of words underneath; one word described the picture while the others did not. Students displayed their completed puzzles to the class and took turns guessing the answers to each other's games. Creating the games was personally affirming to the children, and playing them built community in the classroom. The second week the children created a new set of games using pictures and sentences describing them. Each sentence was left incomplete and followed by a list of possible endings; the object of the game was to choose the appropriate word to complete the sentence. During the third week children combined pictures and sentences again to create another set of games, this time consisting of a picture and four sentences, only one of which accurately described the picture.

6 Let's Get Acquainted
Exercises That Help Remember Names

Remembering names is difficult, especially at the beginning of each school year. The same holds true in any new group situation. The following activities help people learn each other's names in a fun, supportive atmosphere. These games are affirming for participants and help to develop a sense of community. For these reasons, you can use these exercises throughout the year even though their chief purpose is to help remember names. Use the activities and variations which suit your own situation best.

Introductory Name Game Have everyone sit in a circle to foster group feeling and to allow everyone to see and pay attention to the person speaking. Ask a simple, interesting question: "What is your favorite dessert? What is a sport you enjoy? What is your favorite soup?" Go around the circle and have everyone say his or her name and answer the question. Participation should be voluntary; some people may choose not to answer the question. At the beginning questions shouldn't be too personal. Children often prefer to talk about things that are outside of school.

The Memory Name Game is more challenging. It is fairly easy to do if children already know each other. The structure is the same as that used in the *Introductory Name Game* except that children are asked to repeat what each person before them has replied. It is important to ask just one simple question, such as "What is your favorite food?" so that the last person in the circle has a chance of remembering and repeating what everyone else has said. Since there is much repetition, this is an excellent exercise for not only remembering names, but also for learning about each person in a group.

The Find-a-Rhyme Name Song is a good introductory exercise for young children. The song is developed by adding the name of a child in the class to the end of each of the first three lines and then making up a last line that rhymes with the name (see next page). It is a good idea to have a guitar or piano accompaniment when singing this song.

While it is helpful to make up lines in advance, remember that some children are good at improvising. Allow them to make up their own rhymes about one another, while taking care that an atmosphere develops so that no one is put down. It is best if everyone's name is mentioned, but if there are too many in the class to permit this, use the concluding verse shown on the next page.

Find-a-Rhyme Name Song

I know a per-son by the name of [Pe-ter] know a person by the name of [Pe-ter] I know a person by the name of [Pe-ter]. There is no one that is sweeter.

Concluding verse:

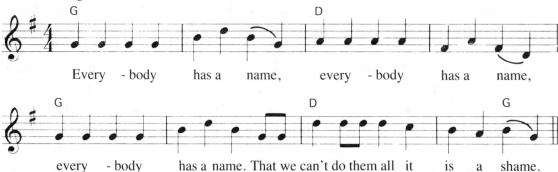

Every-body has a name, every-body has a name, every-body has a name. That we can't do them all it is a shame.

The Introduce-Your-Neighbor Game helps people learn something about other persons in a group. Have everyone sit in a circle. Ask people to form pairs and then take turns talking about themselves. Be sure to announce the half-time mark after two or three minutes, at which time the other person in the pair takes a turn. Then have everyone return to the large circle to introduce his or her partner to the whole group. It is preferable to have people introduce partners voluntarily since this involves more direct participation. If this is awkward, go around the circle for introductions.

For people who prefer more structure, ask a specific question such as "What are three things you like to do?" Give people a chance to think for a minute and then ask them to form pairs. Examples are helpful for getting people started: "In the summer I like to ride horses. In the winter I like to play in the snow."

Introducing Yourself through a Puppet is a game young people play naturally, especially after making puppets. Have the class sit in a circle and pass around a puppet; each child takes a turn introducing herself or another with the puppet. Keep the tempo upbeat; introductions should be fun. For younger children or those unfamiliar with puppets, the exercise is a good introduction to puppetry.

Animal Name Tags helps people in a large group to get to know each other. Provide each child with a name tag with his or her name on it, or leave the tags blank and allow children to fill in their own names. Ask people to draw or put the name of their favorite animal (or simply one animal they like) on the tag. Then, sitting in a circle, each person takes a turn sharing her name, favorite animal, and one thing she likes about her animal. Another possibility is to ask each person to choose an animal most like him or her. This introductory exercise encourages people to laugh and get to know each other with ease.

Three Question Interview is a technique which helps people to learn several things about participants. This is especially effective in a group of parents or teachers who don't know each other well, though it can also be used with children and adults who are familiar with each other. Provide each person with paper and pencil. Have the participants form pairs, preferably with someone they don't know very well. They are to ask each other three simple questions, such as "What is a movie you enjoyed recently?" or "What is one place you would like to visit?" The person asking the questions can jot down his partner's responses. When both people have had a chance to ask three questions, they find other partners and repeat the process. After fifteen to twenty minutes, or when each person has had a chance to interview several others, everyone returns to the large circle. The facilitator goes around the circle and for each person says, "This is ——. What do people know about ——?" People who interviewed that person share what they learned, either from memory or by referring to their notes. Allow time for each person to have a turn. This is an especially affirming exercise for introducing people to each other.

7 Freeing Ourselves Up
Loosening-up Activities

Children placed in groups for the first time are often nervous because they don't know what to expect. Loosening-up activities relieve some of the tension by encouraging them to laugh, act playfully and have fun. Loosening-up activities also increase the energy level in a group and focus children's attention on what is happening.

The Loosening-up Game is a simple theatre warm-up exercise which creates a high energy level and prepares children for skits and role-playing. Stand in front of the group and ask children to imitate the sounds and motions you make. The sillier you look, the more comfortable and low-risk is the atmosphere you produce. After children understand how the exercise works, have others lead with sounds and motions.

The Mirror Exercise is a good follow-up to the *Loosening-up Game*. In the *Mirror,* two children try to imitate each other's actions simultaneously. First one person leads, then the other, but in the final "mirror" both people contribute to the motion. Maintaining eye contact and smooth, flowing motions are helpful; choppy motions are difficult to follow. Begin by demonstrating the *Mirror* yourself, then ask children to pair up, making sure everyone has a partner. Afterwards, ask the children how they felt doing the exercise. The *Mirror* is also an excellent cooperation activity. A variation of this exercise is to have a small group mirror an individual or another group.

The Rebound Exercise can follow the *Mirror,* but have children change partners so more people have a chance to work together. The *Rebound Exercise* allows people to respond back and forth to each other's sounds and motions. One person starts with an action, which can be a combination of sound and motion. The other person "rebounds" with a reaction which is also a new action for the first person to respond to.

Human Protractor   Have everyone stand in a large circle with hands touching toes. While counting from one to twenty, children gradually raise their arms so that by twenty, their hands are reaching towards the sky. Tell children to remember where their hands were at different numbers. Then call out numbers between one and twenty while the group assumes the position for each number. Children love leading this energizing game. It builds community because everyone does the same thing together. For younger children (first and second graders) use it as a counting game and call it *One-to-Ten*.

20

The Mirror Exercise

Human Protractor

21

One-to-Ten Math Game Instead of calling out numbers, the leader calls out addition and subtraction problems. For example, the leader calls out "ten minus two." The others respond "eight" and assume that position. You can play this game using whatever range of numbers are most appropriate for the group. It turns math lessons into fun and group-building activities. Rotate the leader so everyone receives affirmation from the group.

Hand Positions to Tell Time Have children imitate a clock using their arms as the hour and minute hands, making sure others can distinguish the two, while others take turns guessing the time displayed. This is an exciting way to teach children how to use clocks to tell time.

Mask Passing is a theatre warm-up exercise which helps people feel comfortable doing pantomimes and skits. It is fun for all ages, but young children especially enjoy it. Form a circle and demonstrate an unusual expression on your face. "Pass" that expression to the person next to you, who tries to imitate the expression and transform it into a new one. That person passes the new expression to the next one, continuing until everyone in the circle has had a turn. Some groups may be uncomfortable with this exercise, particularly older children and adults.

Herman-Hermina is a good follow-up to *Mask Passing* since it also uses a large circle and is a more complicated pantomime game. Pull "Herman" or "Hermina," an imaginary lump of clay from your pocket and mold an object by means of pantomime. The identity of the object should be simple and clear, so that people understand the game and it gets underway quickly. There is no need to instruct children to guess what each person is making from the clay; their natural curiosity will cause them to guess. Introducing Herman and Hermina silently and treating them with respect heightens the sense of magic surrounding them, creating a make-believe world which children especially love. Though children may want a second or third turn, it is best to end the game after one go-round. Ending a game at its peak brings positive energy to the next activity. If any children did not participate the first time, go around a second time to give them a chance.

Pantomime This Object Young children especially like this game. Choose a real object, such as a broom, and use it to pantomime something else; a guitar, a horse, a violin, etc. Then pass the object around the circle and have children pantomime something with it. Children come up with endless variations. The pantomimed objects are fun to guess, and the game affirms the one taking a turn. Be sure the object you choose has enough possibilities.

Occupation Pantomime Children take turns pantomiming an occupation while others guess what the occupation is. Describe this game by pantomiming an occupation rather than explaining it verbally. The game builds confidence and unifies the group as everyone's attention is focused on each child in turn. The

22

game complements a unit on occupations and helps children to build their vocabularies.

What Kind of Store Is This? is a more difficult pantomime game. Give children time to think of a store to pantomime. Then go around the circle and have children pantomime their choices. Children love to guess each other's pantomimes. This game goes well with the *Group Cooperation Drawing of a Store* (see page 28) or a unit on stores and occupations.

Challenge Pantomime is another difficult pantomime game which older children especially enjoy. Ask a volunteer to go to the center of the circle. Then describe a difficult situation to pantomime: "It is ninety-nine degrees outside and you are trying to eat a double-decker ice cream cone," or "You are walking through three feet of snow carrying a cup of hot cocoa," or "You are walking along and suddenly the floor is covered with marbles." Do this game after children have gained experience with simpler pantomime exercises.

Follow the Sound is a good group-building and loosening-up game. One child in the circle starts by making a sound. His/her neighbor imitates the sound and passes it along. The sound continues around the circle. *Follow the Sound* can also be played with one person in front of the class making sounds which everyone imitates in unison.

Pass the Sound is similar to *Mask Passing*. One person makes a sound and passes it to the next person, who imitates the sound, gradually transforms it and passes it on. The process continues until everyone in the circle has had a turn. This game is personally affirming as well as unifying for the whole group.

Guess the Sound   Each person in a circle makes a sound in turn, while others guess what the sound is. The structure is similar to *Pantomime This Object* and *Herman-Hermina*. Use *Guess the Sound* with a science unit on sounds or as a listening exercise. If children take turns in the middle of the circle or in front of the class, the game is even more affirming.

Light-and-Livelies to Relax and Change Pace

The Philadelphia Nonviolence and Children Program calls the following exercises *light-and-livelies*. They are generally shorter than the loosening-up activities and are ideal after discussions or when children have been sitting for a long while. They are positive, group-building games which lead to laughter and fun. These exercises and others are found in Marta Harrison's excellent handbook, *For the Fun of It*, described in the bibliography.

Zoom is a large circle game which encourages laughter. Imagine the sound of a racing car—*zoom!* Start by saying *zoom* and turning your head quickly to either side of the circle. The person on that side passes the *zoom* to the next person, and so on until everyone has passed the *zoom* around the circle. Next explain that the word *eek* makes the car stop and reverse direction; whenever *eek* is said, the *zoom* goes the opposite way around the circle. At first it is helpful to allow only one *eek* per person to prevent the *eeks* and *zooms* from concentrating in one area of the circle. Later try discarding the rule and encouraging cooperation by making the children responsible for getting the *zoom* all the way around the circle. If the group isn't too large, it is a good idea to continue the game until everyone has had a chance to say *eek*, otherwise everyone who did not say *eek* can do it together.

Elephant and Palm Tree Begin with everyone standing in a circle. One child stands in the middle, points to someone and calls out "elephant" or "palm tree." The "elephant" leans over, clasping his hands together and swinging his arms to form the "trunk." The child to the left becomes the elephant's "left ear," raising her left elbow and touching the top of her head with her hand. The person to the right of the "elephant" does the same with his right arm to form the elephant's "right ear." The "palm tree" stands with arms straight up to form the "trunk." Children to either side hold up their outside arms, hands drooping, to make "fronds." Other variations include *1776* with a fife, drum and flag. It is fun for people to make up their own versions of this game.

Touch Blue is a fun, group-building light-and-lively. Begin by asking people to touch something blue on another person. Then try variations: touch sneakers, touch red hair, touch a wristwatch, touch brown, etc.

Human Jigsaw Puzzle Clear a large space in the center of the room. Have one child lie flat on the floor with arms and legs in any position. Then have other children join the "puzzle," everyone fitting in where they see space. When everyone has joined, ask children to try to memorize the entire puzzle. Next, have everyone get up and walk around a bit. Then try to re-assemble the puzzle with everyone resuming their original positions. This group-building game evokes much laughter.

Human Pretzel is similar in purpose and structure to *Human Jigsaw Puzzle*. Ask children to hold hands firmly and move about, becoming totally entangled like a pretzel. When the knot is completed, ask someone to untangle the pretzel. Throughout the exercise, hands should never be separated.

I Love Ya' Honey but I Just Can't Smile Children sit in a circle for this laughter-producing light-and-lively. Begin by asking the child to your right or left, "Do you love me honey?" He or she responds, "Yes, I love ya' honey, but I just can't smile." The first child then attempts to make the second smile. This continues around the circle until the first person is asked "Do you love me honey?" and is made to smile.

Crazy Faces Big and Small Ask children to make their faces as big as they can and then as small as they can. Repeat this a few times. This activity releases tension and encourages laughter.

Elephant and Palm Tree

Human Pretzel

Jump-in Exercise   Ask children to jump into the circle in a way that expresses themselves. Afterwards, ask the participants how they felt. If children jump in one at a time, the exercise is personally affirming, and if everyone jumps in together, it is more group-building.

My Bonnie   Everyone sings the song "My Bonnie Lies Over the Ocean." Whenever words beginning with a *b* are sung, children alternate between sitting and standing. For example:

> My Bonnie [stand] lies over the ocean
> My Bonnie [sit] lies over the sea

This game is very active; some children may not be able to finish the song or keep up with the rapid sitting and standing. It is so silly that it gets people laughing right away, serving as a good energizer and tension reliever.

8 Let's Build Community
Learning to Cooperate

In our competitive society children rarely have the opportunity to experience successful cooperation. *Cooperation exercises* are structured experiences which provide opportunities for children to work together toward some goal. Cooperation exercises develop a positive atmosphere and encourage individual affirmation and growth. In a cooperative environment, creative conflict resolution can take place. As in other activities, each child should have a chance to participate and should respect the contributions of others.

Cooperation Drawing in Groups

The following exercises show that drawings created by children working together can be as exciting as those made by an individual. In these exercises, encourage children to cooperate not only in the activity of drawing but also in the decision-making process leading up to it. Have children share ideas before they begin drawing. Use large sheets of drawing paper and emphasize the cooperative process rather than the final product. The exercises also enhance children's self-esteem when drawings are shared with the entire class for positive feedback.

Group Cooperation Blackboard Drawing   Choose an appropriate subject, such as the neighborhood around the school. Before beginning, suggest a few ground rules:

–Draw only one thing in proportion to the rest of the drawing.
–No more than five children at the board at one time.
–Think of what you want to draw beforehand so that others don't have to wait long for their turn.

After the drawing is completed, the whole class can look at it, discuss it, and tell how they felt working on it. Ask questions such as "Can anyone see something that someone else added to?"

Group Cooperation Drawing of a Desert Island   Ask children to think about the following question: "If you were on a desert island, what things would you want there to be on the island?" Then divide into small groups and ask children to share their answers. Next, have children each choose one thing to draw and cooperatively decide how to organize their drawings on one sheet of paper. After everyone has finished, ask if anything else should be added. Groups can share their drawings with the rest of the class for affirmation.

Group Cooperation Drawing of a City Block can be done at the blackboard or in small groups. Ask children what they would like to see on a city block. In small groups, have children share their ideas and decide together what to draw. In large groups follow the procedure for *Group Cooperation Blackboard Drawing*.

Group Cooperation Drawing of a Store is appropriate for large or small groups. Ask the following questions to get the drawing process started:

–What kind of store do you want to draw?
–Can the store be drawn easily by a group?
–What are the different parts of the store?
–What part do you want to draw?

After sharing ideas have children begin drawing. You can do this exercise in conjunction with the pantomime game *What Kind of Store Is This* (see page 23) or with a unit on stores and occupations.

Cooperative Monster Making is a drawing exercise best done in groups of five or six. It encourages the expression of vivid imagination. The figures children create can be thought of as monsters, beings from outer space, animals that didn't make it on the ark, or imaginary creatures. Tell the children they won't be judged for artistic ability so the drawings can't be wrong. The more horrible the drawing, the better the monster. There are several ways for children to choose the part of the body they will draw. The quickest is picking names from a hat; children can swap parts if they want to. More challenging is for children to decide cooperatively how to divide up the parts. Allowing children to draw whatever part they want promotes creativity. Remember that a monster can have more than one head and only one foot.

Have plenty of colored construction paper, crayons and scissors available. Staplers work well for putting the parts together. Add drama to the activity by having the children close their eyes while the monsters are being mounted for display. End the exercise by having children share one thing they like about the monsters or discussing how they felt making them.

Other exciting activities can develop from *Cooperative Monster Making*. The following anecdote illustrates what one class did with the idea. At P.S. 75 in upper Manhattan, the principal, Luis Mercado, and two teachers, Louisa and Robert Fuentes, felt that the drawings done for *Cooperative Monster Making* were exceptionally creative. The Fuentes combined their classes to expand the idea and create *El Mundo Imaginario (The Imaginary World)*.

Some students applied ideas from a course on fantasy and film and came up with creatures such as birds, fish and butterflies, as well as some which fit no category.

The children were encouraged to use their full imaginations, with the emphasis that there was no right or wrong. Children discussed what made the monsters strange or special, and these discussions developed into creative writing projects with children writing stories about the monsters.

When *El Mundo Imaginario* was exhibited in school, other classes were excited and made their own creatures. Some decided to make films and videotapes. The idea was so well received that Louisa and Robert Fuentes wrote a book describing the concept, *A Step Further*, which included photographs and writings of the children. *El Mundo Imaginario* was later exhibited at the Bone Hollow Arts Center in Accord, New York.

In addition to activities described in *El Mundo Imaginario*, you can plan a *Storytelling* about the monsters. For more details see *Storytelling*, page 32. The story can be tape-recorded, edited and presented to other classes or used as background material for a play about monsters to perform for other classes.

Snowflakes   Have children make snowflakes by folding paper into eight parts and cutting out designs to resemble snowflakes. When everyone is finished, put all the snowflakes together to form one large "class-size" snowflake. It is exciting to see something beautiful which everyone has contributed to. Another way of doing this exercise is to form small groups which cooperatively creative their own snowflakes.

Group Cooperation Drama Games

Another way to build a sense of community is through drama games. These are even more group building than group cooperation drawings since they involve children working together physically. They are relaxing and involve a lot of moving around and laughing. These exercises help establish a safe atmosphere where children can share feelings openly.

Group Pantomimes   In a circle describe a situation which requires a large group to work together. For example, a pantomime of Grand Central Station at rush hour requires cooperation to create a crowded scene. Another example is a pantomime of a skating scene.

Occupation Pantomime in Groups   Have children form small groups and choose an occupation to pantomime for the whole class. Everyone should have a say in the choice of the occupation and a part to play in the pantomime. When the pantomimes are ready, present them to the whole class and have others guess what the occupations are. This exercise works well with a unit on occupations, along with the individual *Occupation Pantomime, My Favorite Occupation*, and *Affirmation Notebooks*, described in chapter eleven.

Room Building   This exercise works well after children have gained experience with simpler pantomime games. Begin by designating the limits of a room and the location of the door. Children must go through the doorway when entering the room. Each child pantomimes an object in the room while others guess what it is and remember its location so that two objects do not occupy the same space. Objects may be added to already existing objects (a vase may be put on a table, a flower in the vase, food in the refrigerator, and so on). After everyone has had a turn, see if the class remembers all the objects in the room.

Group Cooperation Flowers works in large or small groups. Children create imaginary flowers by positioning each other to resemble flowers. Others can guess what kind of flowers they are, photograph them or draw pictures of them. The object of the exercise is to create something beautiful together.

Cooperative Spelling   The object of this game is to spell words with children in the shape of letters. Children can spell words standing up but it is more fun and effective lying down. *Cooperative Spelling* is an activity for the whole class or groups whose members cooperate to form words and present them to others to guess. It is also an exciting way to practice spelling.

Machine Building can be done in large or small groups. With small groups, begin by demonstrating a "human machine." For example, a washing machine is formed by two people holding hands with arms outstretched and a third person moving around inside as the laundry. Other possibilities include a typewriter, a car wash, or a blender. After the demonstration, form small groups and have children create their own machines for others to guess. Have groups think about the following questions:

   –What machine do you want to build?
   –Is it possible to create the machine with the group?
   –What are the parts of this machine?
   –What part do you want to be?
   –Is the machine complete?

Give children time to rehearse their machines. This activity is affirming as well as group building for the "inventors" of the machines.

   With large groups *Machine Building* is a high-energy exercise which unifies the class. Begin by announcing "We're going to build a machine that we're all part of. When you see a place to fit in, add a sound or motion, or both. Make sure you are connected to another part of the machine." This exercise builds trust and positive feelings.

One-Word Storytelling is a cooperation game for large groups. Someone begins a story with a word, the next one adds a word, and so on around the circle. This short and amusing game encourages children to cooperate by choosing words easy to follow with others or end with.

Cooperative Spelling

Machine Building

31

Storytelling is a community-building exercise for large groups. Begin the story: "Once there were a boy and a girl walking down a very long road. The girl had a basket in her hand…" Clap your hands and point to someone to continue the story. Not knowing who is next keeps interest higher than going around a circle. Children may be called more than once. If there is time, everyone who wants to should have a chance to contribute. The story can be make-believe or realistic; in either case it should move quickly. The more children in the group, the briefer each part should be.

Grab Bag Dramatics is a cooperation game for small groups. Ahead of time prepare paper bags filled with unrelated objects; have one bag for every group, each with one object for every child in the group. Each child takes an object from the bag without looking. After everyone has chosen, children create a skit together which uses all of the objects. It is a good idea to do a demonstration skit in front of the class first. When the skits are ready, groups take turns performing them for the class. You can have children discuss how they put together their skits, or videotape the procedure of one group and play it back for the class to stimulate discussion on the process of cooperation.

Group Cooperation Projects

In these exercises children cooperate to produce something special. They enable children to feel proud of their individual contributions while developing a sense of cohesiveness working together toward a final goal.

Cooperation Fruit Salad   In this activity children create a fruit salad that is later shared with the class. Ask everyone to bring some fruit to class, or assign a specific fruit to each child, or have children count off by apples-pears-bananas-oranges-melons-peaches. Also indicate who will prepare each fruit for the salad and don't forget the cups and spoons. This activity can be used as a fundraising project for the school or as a gift to other classes.

Group Cooperation Sound Effects Tape   Have children think up interesting sounds for a sound effects tape. Have each child choose a sound to record. Possibilities include running water, traffic noise, a school bell, clapping, a siren and whistling. Have children pair up to record the sounds; afterward each group plays back their tape for the rest of the class. Another procedure is to have the class make a single sound effects tape out of contributions from individuals or pairs. The tapes can lead to a discussion of what sound is and the different kinds of sound. This exercise goes well with a science unit.

Group Cooperation Slide Shows   Collect slides that no one wants. Use liquid bleach to remove the pictures: slides with plastic frames can be immersed in bleach, but use a brush or cloth for slides with cardboard frames. Give each child a cleaned slide and fine-pointed markers. Ask children to make a design on the slide and put their name on the frame. Put the slides together and have a class slide show. Small groups can also put together mini-slide shows and add music and a script. A few members of the class may want to share the slide shows with other classes and teach them how to make their own. Producing slide shows is an affirming and satisfying cooperative activity.

Cooperative Building with Tinkertoys works best in small groups. There are two ground rules:

(1) Everyone participates in deciding what to build; and

(2) Everyone contributes to the building.

Have children form small groups to build something cooperatively with Tinkertoys. After groups have finished their buildings, have everyone reassemble to share and discuss their creations. Older children may discuss how they worked together. It is helpful to have a facilitator for each group.

Other Group Cooperation Activities

The following exercises are joyful games that children can play in large groups during the day. They build a sense of community while providing fun and positive experiences for children.

Rainstorm is a circle game in which children simulate the sounds of a rainstorm. The facilitator begins by rubbing hands together in front of one child in the circle. That child imitates the sound, and the facilitator moves on adding children one-by-one into the sound. Children continue rubbing hands while the facilitator makes a second pass around the circle, this time snapping fingers in front of each child. On the next pass the facilitator makes a pattering sound on the legs. The peak of the storm occurs with feet stamping. So far the wind has rustled the leaves, and the rain has begun, grown louder and developed into a full thunder storm. Now the storm subsides. The stamping feet are followed by the pattering legs, then the clicking fingers and finally the rubbing hands, getting quieter and quieter until there is silence.

Community Music Making can be performed with handmade instruments (see chapter twelve), kazoos, harmonicas, tambourines, recorders, guitars, spoons, sticks, bottles, jugs or pans. Form a circle and give each child an instrument. Choose someone to conduct and remind children that in an orchestra the musicians pay careful attention to the conductor. The conductor begins by pointing to one musician to play. After a rhythm is established, the conductor points to the next person and waits for the sound to develop before continuing around the circle until everyone is part of the music making. When the mood is cooperative and serious, the music can be remarkably good and affirming.

Children often enjoy playing for a long time. To take advantage of this, use variations such as pointing to children for solos or duets. The conductor can also direct similar instruments to play together.

Community Music Making

Scavenger Hunt encourages cooperation in small groups. Assemble a number of packets containing materials and instructions for using them in a cooperative activity. Hide these packets in different parts of the school such as the library, gym and lunchroom (be sure to consult teachers in those areas beforehand). Send groups of children out on a scavenger hunt to locate the packets and follow the enclosed instructions. Here are some suggested activities:

–Imagine it is a rainy day. Draw a picture of what you as a group want to do.
–Make paper bag puppets and put on a show.
–Build something together out of these tinkertoys.
–Share these cookies.
–Tell a story which everyone in the group contributes to.

There can be a surprise at the end or a time to share what each group did. Either way, it is important to emphasize cooperation rather than winning the scavenger hunt.

Magic Microphone is an exercise that facilitates group discussion. Choose an object that is large enough to see and small enough to pass around. This object is the magic microphone. When someone has it, it is that child's special time to talk. Children cooperate by sharing the microphone. It is important to treat it with respect.

Musical Laps is a noncompetitive version of musical chairs. Children stand in a circle holding on to the waist of the child in front of them. When the music plays, children walk around in the circle, and when it stops, they sit down in the lap behind them. If children cooperate, everyone has a comfortable lap to sit on. If they do not sit down gently or provide others with a seat, then the whole circle falls down. Children love this game and try very hard to keep the circle up.

Singing is a positive, group-building activity to bring children together, close a special time, energize or relieve tension in a group. See the appendix for songs that children especially enjoy.

9 Do You Hear Me?
Learning to Communicate

Conflict and violence frequently occur when there is lack of communication. It is difficult to deal with a problem if we do not understand it, and it is hard to understand it if we are unable to hear what other people are saying. Often we make assumptions about others that turn out to be untrue. Improving our observation skills helps us to understand why conflicts occur. Improving our speaking skills gives us the chance to practice communicating to assess how well we are understood by others.

Listening Skills

The following games and exercises help children to practice and improve their listening skills in a fun and supportive atmosphere. They also encourage children to think about what communication is and what interferes with communication.

The Telephone Game usually highlights problems in communication. The message received by the last person differs from the original in an amusing way. When this game is used to improve listening skills, it is played in a different way. The goal is to have the last child receive the original message accurately by analyzing how messages get around. Sit in a circle and begin with a simple sentence, such as "Last night the moon was shining and I loved watching it." Pass the message around the room in a whisper. More likely than not, it will be garbled by the time it reaches the last child. Ask children what helps them to hear the message correctly. Answers may include speaking into the listener's ear, speaking slowly and clearly, a quiet room, etc. List children's answers on the blackboard. Think of a new message and go around the circle again. Make the length and difficulty of the message appropriate for the group. If the final message differs from the original, resume the discussion using the list generated earlier. Go around the circle a third time and tell children to check back if the message is unclear. They may ask, "Did you say ——" and the other child may reply, "Yes, I said ——." Checking back should enable children to pass around the message successfully. This game is a group-building way to improve children's listening skills.

Telegraph is similar to the *Telephone Game* except that the message is nonverbal and instead consists of squeezes and pauses sent through the hands. Have children

The Telephone Game

close their eyes so no one can see the message. Children hold hands in a circle, which makes this game a unifying experience. After the message goes around the circle, the last child explains verbally what it was. The message can also be sent in both directrions until one child receives it from both sides, especially in large groups. You can use *Telegraph* with a history unit and have children pretend to send a message from New York to California and back. Another variation is to send messages using the Morse code.

Cooper Says is a cooperative version of *Simon Says* which helps children to improve their listening skills in a fun atmosphere. Children stand arm's length apart facing Cooper and follow directions only when preceded by "Cooper says." The game differs from "Simon Says" because children remain in the game even when they do something Cooper did not tell them to. This lowers the risk level and involves more children in the game. One variation is to challenge the whole class to follow ten directions accurately. Cooper loves to see cooperation, the first six letters of which spell his name!

Communication Storytelling is a cooperation and listening game for small groups. Children sit in a circle and take turns contributing to a story until everyone has added to it. It is fun to tape record the stories and play them back to see if each contribution was heard and the story held together. Be sure that each group has a working tape recorder. An interesting variation is to have one group pantomime another group's story. Children may also want to play stories to another class or turn them into a book.

The Description Game encourages children to listen closely to each other. Have three children give different descriptions of the same object without naming it. The object described should be fairly complex and visible to everyone else. Have the rest of the class use the three descriptions to identify the object. A bulletin board, for example, may be described as something with pictures or writing on it. Some descriptions may be general, others very specific. The *Description Game* improves listening skills by encouraging children to concentrate on what others say. It is also an observation game which teaches children to focus on the details of an object. The *Description Game* can lead to a discussion of how everyone sees things differently. You can also use it as a creative writing exercise.

Direction Following works best in a large group. Have three children listen carefully to a set of directions that are given only once. One by one each child takes a turn following the directions while the class observes whether or not the directions are followed. Allow all three to finish before having the class share observations. The directions should be fairly complicated but not too long. For example, "Go to the blackboard, write your name three times, put an *X* to the right of the second name and underline the third name. Go to the window, clap your hands three times, return to your seat, sit down, cross your legs and shake hands with the child to your left." Children following directions must listen very carefully in order to succeed, while the rest of the class must both listen and observe to know if the directions are followed. One variation is to use small groups so everyone has a chance to both follow directions and observe. Use the game to stimulate a discussion on the importance of giving clear directions as well as listening to them.

Paraphrasing is a challenging activity for children. Pick a topic that is relevant to the group. Have someone talk about it and others take turns paraphrasing what was said. Explain that paraphrasing is using different words to express what someone else has said. Each child's paraphrase must be approved by the original speaker before the next person takes a turn. Everyone should talk on the same topic. This game can also be played in small groups with observers. Either way, *Paraphrasing* is a serious game which actively improves listening skills.

Listening Time helps children practice listening and is also an excellent way to begin an activity since it focuses everyone's attention in a quiet way. Start by asking children to listen to the sounds outside the room. After a minute or so have children share what they heard. *Listening Time* shows how much children can hear when they are quiet.

Observation Skills

Many of the following games are similar to the listening exercises but the emphasis is on seeing rather than hearing. These games develop useful skills for analyzing why conflict occurs and stimulate discussion of body language, facial expression and other forms of nonverbal communication.

The Open-Closed Game is an exciting way to introduce the theme of observation. Sit in a circle and explain that in this observation game children must look closely for clues to tell whether a book you will pass around is "open" or "closed." The clue is that when your legs are apart the book is "open," and when your legs are crossed the book is "closed," even though in reality the book may be open. When children understand the object of the game, begin passing around the book. Each child says "I am passing the book to you open" if her/his legs are apart or "I am passing the book to you closed" if his/her legs are crossed. Pass the book around the circle until most children have discovered the clue. Take care to provide simple and clear instructions to this game. Having children feel successful at the game is as important as improving observation skills. Children experienced with observation games may want to create more difficult versions of the *Open-Closed Game*.

The Magician Game helps children practice concentration and observation of details. While one child dresses up in an exotic outfit as the Magician, another announces to the class the arrival of a surprise visitor who can guess the identity of any object the children secretly pick. The class chooses three objects in the room. Be sure to say there is a reason the magician can guess what they are thinking, and if children concentrate they can discover the magician's secret. Introduce the magician to the class with great reverence and begin asking questions: "Is the object the students have chosen Dale's green sweater? Is it the math book on the desk?" The magician and the facilitator have chosen beforehand one object (for instance, the teacher's desk), and when the facilitator names that object, the magician knows the next object is the one chosen by the class. After several rounds children should be able to discover the secret. Follow with a discussion. The secret should be challenging, but not impossible for children to figure out. This enjoyable introduction to observation skills can serve as a reference point for later, more serious work.

The Eyewitness Skit is another dramatic way to develop observation skills. The goal is to show how everyone sees things from a different perspective. Ahead of time have some children prepare a skit containing details that will be challenging for others to recall. Do not announce the skit but have them present it to the class in an attention-grabbing way. It should be clear to everyone that it is a skit and not a real-life situation. Have children discuss what happened. There will probably be several different versions of the events. Have children try to explain the differences (children were in different parts of the room, there was too much noise, and so on). Make a list of such reasons and refer to it whenever communication problems arise in the classroom.

Skits to Observe for Detail   This activity is a variation on the *Eyewitness Skit* for small groups. Using the same rules have a group of children illustrate the procedure with a sample skit for the class. Divide the class into small groups and have each group prepare a detailed skit to perform in front of the others. Have children share observations after each skit. While the purpose of the skits is to improve observation skills, they are also confidence building and unifying for the whole class.

Know Your Orange is a fascinating game which helps children develop an eye for minute detail. In a circle, pass out one orange to each child. Tell everyone they will have five minutes to examine their oranges carefully. The oranges will be collected, shuffled and placed in the center of the circle, and each child will have to find his or her orange! Children should be able to recognize their oranges easily. A more challenging version is to have children locate their oranges with their eyes closed. Discuss what makes it possible to distinguish one orange from all the rest. All oranges are not alike! You can substitute potatoes, apples or any other inexpensive produce.

The Fishbowl combines speaking, listening and observing skills. In this exercise children observe an activity taking place in the center of the circle or "fishbowl." Divide the group into two concentric circles. The fishbowl activity can be either a conversation or a roleplay. Topics may include planning a class trip, a game booth for a street carnival, or a party for the last day of school. Older children may want to discuss a certain problem in the school, but avoid highly controversial topics which will distract children from observing the process. To help children to focus on the process, use the following checklist.

Observer Checklist
–Did everyone speak?
–Did everyone listen?
–Was anyone prevented from speaking by others?
–Were children fidgety or restless?
–Were children looking at the speaker?
–Did everyone speak loudly and clearly?
–Did speakers address everyone in the group or just a few?
–Did the group stick to the topic?

Read aloud each of these questions to the whole class. Ask children to paraphrase the questions so they have a clear understanding of them. Emphasize that answering the questions is not as important as working together to observe what is happening in the fishbowl. After the activity in the fishbowl ends, ask children how they felt and have children discuss their observations by reviewing the checklist. You can also do a series of fishbowls so everyone has a chance to be in the center of the circle.

The Fishbowl

Rumor develops observation skills. Have a volunteer leave the room. Then show a fairly complicated picture to the rest of the class. Tell them to examine the picture carefully so they can describe it later. Put the picture away and have the volunteer return. Have the class describe what was in the picture; usually there are several different versions. This can lead to a discussion of observation. When this game is played several times in a row, it helps to improve observation skills. A more complicated variation is to have two children leave the room. Bring back one at a time, the first to hear the class describe the picture and the second to hear the first describe what s/he heard from the class. This can turn into a discussion of how rumors get started.

Speaking Skills

Often communication is hindered because children are unable to hear what someone else is saying. Children who do not speak clearly are frequently unaware of this problem. These exercises create a fun, safe atmosphere for children to develop confidence in speaking, some simply by pointing out the need to speak loudly and clearly.

The Inquiring Reporter Interviewing Game helps children build confidence speaking in front of a group. One child plays inquiring reporter who has come to investigate the school and students. The reporter asks someone, "On what subject would you like to be interviewed?" The reporter asks questions on the subject in an official tone and jots down notes. You can hold interviews at intervals throughout the week or in small groups so everyone can be interviewed in one session. In either case attention should be focused on the child being interviewed, since it is his or her special time. The game is both confidence building for the individual and community building for the group. Afterward interviews can be written down on newsprint.

The Diaphragm Breathing Exercise is a good introduction to voice projection. Begin with everyone standing in a large circle. Have children put their hands on their abdomens, take a deep breath and feel their diaphragms expand. Have them exhale and feel their diaphragms contract. Have everyone inhale slowly as you count to ten, until they are breathing from the diaphragm. With hands still on abdomens, have everyone say "ho, ho, ho." If children are speaking from the diaphragm, they should sound loud and be able to feel their diaphragm contract with each "ho." Next go around the circle and have everyone say at least five words from the diaphragm. Use this exercise when children need practice projecting their voices.

The Distance Speaking Game is an exciting way to encourage children to speak loudly and clearly. Before the game, cut strips of crepe paper in two colors so each child has a strip of each color. Explain that the strips are flags to wave to indicate whether they can hear others speaking clearly. ("Wave the brown flag if you can hear, the white flag if you can't.") Divide the class into two teams facing each other across the room. Have one child from each team go to the center of the room to face each other and the side they came from. Choose an interesting topic for the two children to discuss, such as going to the circus or street carnival. Explain that whenever they hear the facilitator clap hands, each child in the center takes one step backward and away from her/his original team. As the children in the center discuss the topic, each team waves its flags to indicate whether or not they can hear. The speakers should be aware of the flags and attempt to speak more clearly. When the speakers have backed up all the way, they join the opposite team and others take their place in the center. It is more comfortable if children have chairs to sit in. Everyone should have a chance to be in the center. If children are bored with the topic, change it to something more interesting to them. Since the game is fairly complicated, be sure to explain carefully all the rules before beginning.

Speaking in Front of the Group is a good way to conclude a unit on speaking skills. Have everyone prepare a talk to deliver to the entire class. Choose topics by drawing suggestions from a hat, or let children choose their own. Have the class behave as an audience by sitting back to add a formal tone to the game. While this is a most challenging exercise, the atmosphere should still be a safe one because everyone knows they are only playing a game.

10 We Are All Special
Affirmation of Ourselves and Others

Poor self-image is at the root of many conflicts in schools. If children do not feel positive about themselves, it is difficult for them to feel positive about others. This inability prevents children from seeing another child's point of view and is the basis of many putdowns.

The following exercises are designed to help children identify positive things about themselves and their peers. These exercises provide children with new experiences that make them feel proud and good about themselves.

The first section of exercises is for large groups, while the second consists of activities to encourage individuals to affirm themselves.

Large Group Affirmation Activities

Affirmation Name Tags   Have children write on a name tag their favorite color, subject or place, or one thing they like about themselves. Afterward go around the circle and share each child's response.

Do a Motion that Expresses Your Name   Begin in a circle and do a motion that expresses your first name, then a motion that expresses your family name. Go around the circle and have children do motions that express their names. In this exercise each child has a chance to be expressive and receive attention. Even more affirming is to have everyone repeat the names and motions. This helps children learn names, encourages laughter, and develops a sense of group.

Pantomime One Thing You Like to Do is group building and personally affirming. In a circle, ask children to pantomime one thing they like to do. Be sure to let each person finish the pantomime before others start to guess. Everyone who wants to do a pantomime should have a chance.

Magic Box is another pantomime game. Place an imaginary magic box in the center of the circle. Each child in turn goes to the box and takes out something, pantomiming an activity or game. When others in the circle guess the activity, they go to the center and join in, and the originator tells them if they are correct. Another child takes something out of the box, and the process continues. The game affirms those in the center of the circle.

The Affirmation Interview is an activity in which one child is interviewed and given attention by the whole group. The questions should be simple, nonthreatening, and interesting. For example:

–What is your favorite sandwich?
–What place would you like to visit?
–What is something you enjoy doing on Saturday morning or after –school?
–What good movie have you seen lately?

The interviewer should look directly at the child being interviewed, and ask questions appropriate to him or her. The interviewer should be positive and praise the child as much as possible. Limit the number of interviews so everyone enjoys an equal amount of attention from the group.

I'm Going on a Trip (and I'm Taking a Hug) encourages the expression of physical affection. Each child in a group adds one expression to what the previous is bringing on the trip: "I'm going on a trip and I'm bringing a hug and a handshake and a pat on the back." The last child in the circle receives everything that the rest of the children are bringing on the trip. This exercise provides a safe way for children to touch. If children are embarrassed by touching and affection, save this exercise for a time when a sense of community has developed.

Word Tickler can be done when children have known each other for awhile. Children pair up and say as many nice things as possible about the other and after a few minutes the partners switch roles. This makes the child being talked about laugh; one is "tickling" the other with words. A more structured version is to have children say three nice things about each other. If the class has done several affirmation exercises, try having each child say one nice thing about his or her neighbor in front of the whole class. All three methods are affirming; choose the best one for your group.

New-And-Goods can be used to begin the day or week, as a small group exercise or to focus the attention of the group. Often at the beginning of a new activity children's thoughts are somewhere else. *New-and-Goods* helps children to focus on a specific question and arouses positive feelings about it. This enables children to collect themselves for a new activity with full attention.

Choose one question to ask the group: "What is one thing good that happened to you recently?" Later vary the questions: "What is your favorite color? Who is one person you admire?" Each person should have a chance to speak and be heard by everyone else. In a large group, the turns should be short, although in the small groups children can spend more time. *New-and-Goods* can also be used with the curriculum: "What is one thing you liked about the story we read?" Or the class might want to compile a new-and-goodspaper where exciting classroom events are recorded on large sheets of newsprint and posted in the classroom. These can be compiled and illustrated by different children each day.

Singing affirms and energizes children and builds community. Songs (listed in the appendix) combined with action are especially affirming. A safe atmosphere encourages more affirmation.

Affirmation Clapping is a birthday exercise which works well with younger children. One child is affirmed by everyone focusing attention on him or her, clapping as follows:

Here is a *clap* for ——.
Here is a *clap* for health.
Here is a *clap* for wealth.
And here is a *clap* for love upon you.
Here is a *clap* for all the years you've grown
And all you have to grow.

Follow the final line with a burst of clapping.

Individual Affirmation Exercises

There are two types of affirmation exercises in this section. In the first, children affirm themselves by creating something they are proud of. In the second, children affirm each other. Both are community building and many of these exercises are compatible with the curriculum.

Silhouettes   Children pair up and trace each other on large sheets of brown wrapping paper. They can fill in features with crayons, paint or magic markers. Bring in plenty of fabric, yarn and glue for clothing and hair. Have children put their names on their silhouettes and hang them on the wall when finished. Have children discuss how they felt creating the silhouettes.

Putting Positive Statements on Silhouettes works best in small groups. Children write their names on index cards and distribute them to each member of the group. Each child writes one nice thing about each person on his or her card. Have children sign their names if they want to. When everyone is finished, the cards are returned and children enjoy their praise. If there is time, go around the circle and have children say one thing they liked about doing the affirmation cards. Collect the cards and tape or paste them to the silhouettes made in the previous exercise. When children feel sad, they can look at their silhouettes and remember all the good things that were said about them. You can also regard this as a reading and writing exercise.

Stocking Fillers   Everyone in the group hangs up a sock or stocking with his or her name on it. Have children write their names on five slips of paper which go into a hat. Everyone draws five slips, writes a positive thing about each one, and puts it into the proper stocking. In a longer version of this game everyone in the class writes something positive about everyone else. Make it clear that putdowns are not allowed.

Affirmation Valentines is a February version of *Stocking Fillers*. Have each child glue three sides of a red heart packet. Children decorate and sign the hearts

46

which are put on the wall. Next have children write their names on two index cards and shuffle them in a hat. Each child draws two cards and writes a positive statement about the child whose name is on the card. If children pick their own or two for the same child, they should pick again. Place the affirmation cards in the heart packets. A good way to end this exercise is to have each child share a statement that was pleasing. Another possibility for an *Affirmation Valentine* is to make a giant class heart on which there is a positive statement about each member of the class. Have children draw names from a hat, write affirmations on the heart and end by sharing something they like about the heart. You can use either version of *Affirmation Valentine* as a reading and writing exercise.

Grab Bag Affirmation Notes is similar to *Stocking Fillers* and *Affirmation Valentines* and can also be used as a reading and writing project. Write each child's name on seven slips of paper and put them in a bag. Each child draws seven slips and writes something positive about the child on each slip. These can be handed to the children, put into affirmation stockings or read aloud. Choose the process best for your group.

Affirmation Video Many schools have portable, easy-to-use video equipment. In *Affirmation Video* each child says one positive thing about himself or herself in front of the camera. If the class is large, keep each child's comment short to maintain interest to the end. It is helpful to give children a chance to think about what they want to say before recording them. For children unfamiliar with affirmation exercises, ask "What is something that makes you smile?" Record children in a quiet corner of the class or a separate room to reduce background noise which may distort the tape. During playback use a large monitor so everyone can see easily. Mention that laughing is fine but putdowns are not allowed. Afterward ask how children felt seeing themselves and others on TV or have them write about it. A variation of this exercise is to have children interview each other in front of the camera.

Affirmation Fortune Cookies and Cupcakes Have each child write one positive fortune. Collect the fortunes and put them inside cookie or cupcake dough to be baked. Pass out the goodies to eat and ask children to discuss how their fortunes relate to them. You can also use this as a reading and writing exercise. Folding the fortunes before placing them in the dough is helpful.

Picture Games

The following activities help children improve vocabulary skills and practice for reading tests by associating words and pictures. The supplies you need are large sheets of paper (one for each child), crayons or magic markers, glue or staplers, scissors and pictures from magazines. Choose pictures beforehand or have children cut them out themselves. The pictures should show something clearly; save more interpretive pictures for creative writing or discussion activities.

Word Game Explain to children that they are going to make up word games using pictures. Ask them to choose a picture that shows one word clearly and to think of three other words that the picture does not show. The picture is pasted alongside the word choices. Be sure children put their names on their papers so they are praised for their work. When the word games are finished, have children share and play each other's games.

Make up a word game in front of the class to clarify the directions. Hold up a picture and ask what it is; then ask for three words that do not name what is in the picture. Write the words on the blackboard. Ask children what the correct answer is. When the directions are clear children can begin. Have children work together so they can help each other with spelling.

This game helps children learn to think of, read and spell words. It also provides a group activity which is affirming to children as they share the word games they create. Stress that this is an activity where everyone shares their word games. Applause after each presentation is affirming to everyone.

Fill-in-the-Blank Word Game is a more complicated picture game which helps children to think about sentence structure. Have children find pictures which show an action. For each picture, children make up a sentence describing the action. Sentences are left blank and followed by a list of possible endings, including the correct one.

Sentence Game is an even more difficult picture game. Ask children to make up four different sentences about a picture, one of which describes accurately what is happening in the picture. All three picture games can be done by children working alone or in small groups. In groups of three or four, children can cooperatively create the games and later share them with the whole class. Younger children may prefer working in small groups or in pairs. Choose what is best for your class.

If My Feet Could Talk is a creative writing exercise which encourages children to think and write about themselves. Children find the idea of talking feet amusing, which makes the writing assignment fun. The idea is similar to talking through puppets; children who have difficulty speaking in groups often are able to do so through another medium. Younger children may have only a few words for their feet to say, while older children may write sentences and paragraphs. After children have written their "feet pieces," they can read them to the class. Others may prefer to have someone else read their piece. Allow children to decide whether to share their work.

Puppets Making puppets is an affirming activity for children. Shy children often will talk freely with puppets, especially with ones that they made.

Sock puppets are easy to make. Have an old sock for each child and scraps of material and yarn. Cut out eyes, mouth, hair, etc., and paste them on the sock

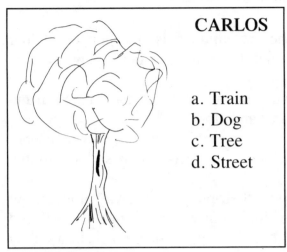

CARLOS

a. Train
b. Dog
c. Tree
d. Street

Word Game

ANDREA

The child is:

a. swimming.
b. running.
c. smiling.
d. writing.

Fill-in-the-Blank Word Game

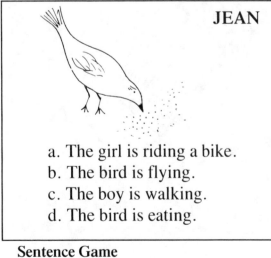

JEAN

a. The girl is riding a bike.
b. The bird is flying.
c. The boy is walking.
d. The bird is eating.

Sentence Game

49

with glue. Be sure to let the glue dry before children use the puppets. Older children may want to sew on features. It is helpful to make a sample puppet for the class group before beginning.

Use paper lunchbags and draw faces with crayons or magic markers. Yarn and fabric can also be glued on to make features and clothes.

Books on more complicated forms of puppet making such as papier-mâché, styrofoam, celastic, rod puppets and shadow puppets are described in the bibliography.

Children may want to say something with their puppets as a way of affirming what they have done. You can also have children give their puppets names and share them with the class. Children do not need scripts to do puppet shows; they love to create their own scenarios and act out stories they make up or have heard. For puppet shows you can use a blanket thrown over a table as a makeshift stage. You can also have children make a permanent puppet stage as a cooperation project.

Although you may want to keep the puppets in the classroom for much of the year for shows on cooperation or conflict resolution, eventually allow children to take their puppets home. Puppets can also be kept in special "homes" around the classroom or in *Affirmation Notebooks*.

11 A Notebook All about Me!
Creating a Treasured Possession

The ***Affirmation Notebook*** is a collection of self-affirming sheets that children create and compile throughout the year. Use the ideas described here to make up blank sheets to reproduce for your class as appropriate. The purpose of these sheets is for children to express positive ideas about themselves. Some sheets encourage self-affirmation through drawing and helping children clarify what they like to do. Others are a personal record of who children are and what is special about them. Still others can be used with curriculum units combining affective and cognitive learning. All of the sheets encourage children to express positive ideas about themselves creatively and to recognize and affirm each other.

It is a good idea to do a sample sheet in front of the class so children are clear about the directions and purpose of each sheet. It is also helpful to hold an evaluation at the end of each activity to share affirmations and build community. Evaluations also give you insight into which sheets your children enjoy most. You can also use the sheets as separate exercises independent of the *Affirmation Notebook*.

The Affirmation Notebook Cover can be made before or after making the individual sheets of the *Affirmation Notebook*. The cover provides a place for children to keep all the sheets they create about themselves.

Each child needs two large sheets of oak tag, crayons, magic markers and brass fasteners. If you punch holes in the oak tag in advance children can fasten the notebooks together right away and avoid confusing the bottom, top, back and front.

Ask children to write their names on the front cover, either simply for identification or as an elaborate design. Next have children draw a symbol that represents themselves, such as a flower, tree, mountain, baseball glove or self-portrait. Children also may trace their hands. Younger children may want to draw a picture of something they like.

The final step is for children to write positive comments on one another's notebook covers. Structure this step so that an equal number of comments is written on each child's notebook. One way is to form small groups and pass the covers around. Children don't have to sign their names to their comments, but those receiving comments usually like it if they do. Another way is to have children write comments on eight different notebooks and point out that each notebook should have only eight comments on it. In a small group where children are already supportive of one another, you can leave it open and have everyone write on as many notebook covers as time permits.

Encourage children to help each other with spelling, drawing and sharing supplies. If someone writes a negative comment, state clearly that this is an affirmation exercise and erase the comment or have the child start over. Be sure to affirm anyone who is put down. In some cases it is helpful to affirm the child who made the negative comment.

Even if you do not plan to do other *Affirmation Notebook* sheets, you can still do this exercise on large sheets of paper. Covers can be displayed in the library or halls.

Drawings

In the following exercises children create affirmative drawings. Make your demonstration pictures simple and easy to draw.

Affirmation T-shirts This exercise encourages children to think about themselves and what they like to do. Draw a picture of a T-shirt and make enough copies for the entire class. Give the following directions:

–Put your name on the sheet.
–Draw a picture of something you like to do.
–Write one word that describes *you*. This word can relate to the picture, but does not have to. For children who have difficulty drawing, suggest using stick figures.

To complete this activity have children describe their pictures or read their words to the class. Children are generally interested in what others have done but be sure to move things along so that those at the end will get their share of attention. Don't force children to share their pictures. At the end simply announce, "If you haven't shown your T-shirt yet, you can do it now." This gives children a second chance if they want one.

Some children will finish early, so plan an activity for them. If children are working in small groups, you can ask children why they chose their symbol and encourage personal sharing. You can expand the T-shirt idea into a project in which children put their symbols on real T-shirts.

My Snow Person is an affirmation sheet for younger children in which they create a drawing they are proud of. Children love to decorate the snow persons like the one below. At the end of the exercise children can share their snow persons and discuss how they felt doing them.

My Very Own Button encourages children to create their own design for a button which can be used later to make a real button.

Affirmation T-Shirts

My Snow Person

One Animal I Like helps children to think about and draw a favorite animal. It can be used with a unit on animals to help young children learn the names of animals; in this case have children write the names on their sheets.

A Map of My Neighborhood is an interesting way for children to learn about maps and communities. For young children you may want to do a map of the classroom. Have children find out the names of their neighborhood streets before doing this exercise.

Self Portrait is one of the most difficult affirmation sheets and should be done when children have developed strong self-concepts. The *Self-Portrait* sheet is reproduced with a blank oval on it and a place for the child's name. Directions are simple: "Put your name on the paper and color in a picture of yourself." Some children may feel more comfortable doing drawings of each other.

Personal Sheets

The following written exercises encourage self-awareness. These sheets help children to learn more about themselves and others in a positive atmosphere and may be regarded as reading or writing projects.

The Balloon Sheet encourages children to look at what they like to do and be affirmed by it. Each child should have a sheet with blank balloons as illustrated on page 55. Give the following directions:

–Put your name on the paper.
–Write one thing you like to do in each balloon. For example: roller skate, eat ice cream or see movies.

–Use crayons, colored pencils, magic markers or pens.

–Some children may want to color the balloons, while others may want to add new ones.

Questions about Me is a good exercise for the beginning of the year to introduce children to each other. Adapt the questions used in the example below to the age-level and interests of the children. Younger children prefer single-word fill-ins; older children usually prefer questions allowing them to describe something in detail. Children may want to make up several *Questions about Me* sheets.

How I Spend My Time helps children look at what they do during the day. Have children fill in clocks with things they do at different hours of the morning, afternoon or evening. This exercise can also be used with a unit on time.

If I Could Do Anything I Wanted for One Week in New York helps children to imagine what they would do if they could do anything they wanted. You can substitute other cities for New York in this writing exercise.

My Family Sheet This sheet can be used with the *Family Tree* exercise that follows. Children enjoy fill-in-the-blank exercises if they are not used as tests. You can use this activity in a unit on families or as a writing and spelling exercise. Adapt the sample sheet to the needs of your class. Some other ideas are:

–On Saturdays we often ———.

–One really good thing about my family is ———.

–The youngest person in my family is ——— and the oldest is ———.

–If my family could do anything for our vacation, we would ———.

After the sheets are filled out, have children share something about their families. In a large group children can read one thing from their sheets. In small groups children can share all or some of the fill-ins. If trust is high, children may discuss the topic, "What I'd like to see changed in my family." Or children may hold a problem-solving discussion to work on one child's problem at a time and try to come up with usable solutions.

The Family Tree is simply a tree with empty boxes attached to the limbs and a circle on the top. Have children put their names in the circle and the names of family members in the boxes. In order to prevent children from feeling that they don't fit in and to encourage them to think about who is part of their families, there are no boxes set aside specifically for the mother, father, etc. Mention that a family can include aunts, uncles, nieces, nephews, cousins, friends, dogs and cats. If children want to, they can write the relationship under the name. You can use this exercise with *My Family* and follow it with a sharing circle on "One thing I like about my family." It can be used as part of a unit on families or as a writing exercise. The *Family Tree* can also go in the *Affirmation Notebook*.

54

My name is

HOW I SPEND MY TIME

a.m.

p.m.

A MAP OF MY NEIGHBORHOOD

My name is _____
My address is _____
_____

Here is a map of my neighborhood:

My name is _____

QUESTIONS ABOUT ME

1. I am _____ years old.
2. I have _____ eyes.
3. I have _____ hair.
4. I live at _____
5. I live with _____
6. My favorite food is _____
7. One color I like is _____
8. An animal I like is _____
9. A song I like is _____
10. My favorite book is _____
11. My favorite TV show is _____
12. A good movie I've seen lately is _____
13. One thing I'm proud of is _____
14. If I could go anywhere I'd go to visit_____
15. My favorite game is _____

My name is _____

**IF I COULD DO ANYTHING
I WANTED FOR
ONE WEEK IN NEW YORK**

First I would _____

_____

Then I would _____

_____
_____
_____
_____

My name is _____

THE BALLOON SHEET

These are things I like to do:

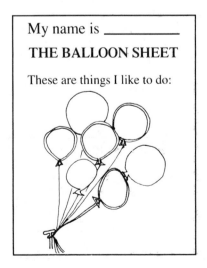

Other Affirmation Notebook Sheets

Photograph Sheet   Take pictures of everyone in the class and have children attach them to notebook sheets. It is a good idea to take two or three shots of each child so they can choose the one they like best. Older children may want to take each other's pictures, or you can invite a parent or friend to be the photographer for the day. You can also take group and/or class pictures. You can combine this exercise with a unit on photography and create a photography exhibit for the classroom, hall or library.

Sheet for Puppets   After children have made puppets (see page 48), have them make an affirmation sheet for their puppets. The sheets can state the name of the child as well as the puppet. When they are finished have children attach the sheets to their puppets.

Use your imagination to develop new sheets for the *Affirmation Notebooks*. Valuable suggestions can come from the children and other teachers. Other possible *Affirmation Notebook* sheets include *Books I Like; TV Shows I Watch; My Favorite Fruit, Recipes I Enjoy, What I Want to Be When I Grow Up, My Favorite School Trip, An Interview with a Friend, The Best Things that Ever Happened to Me, My Earliest Memory,* and *Calendar of Important Dates.* Many of these exercises are applicable to other classroom activities.

My name is _____
FOOD
One food I really like is _____
_____
It looks like this:

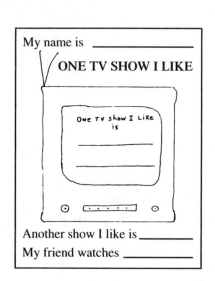

12 Let's Make an Instrument
An Affirming Activity for Everyone

In this activity children feel positive about themselves through their ability to create a musical instrument. Each child can put her name on the instrument she makes and keep it. Have children leave their instruments in the room to use for community music making (see **Cooperation Activities,** page 33), but eventually everyone should be able to take the instrument home. The following are some instruments that children enjoy and take pride in making. (Susi Woodman suggested these.)

Ukulele   For each ukulele you need a quart or half-gallon size milk carton and four rubber bands which fit snugly lengthwise around the carton. Make four notches along the top edge of the milk carton and four similarly spaced notches along the bottom edge. Cut the soundbox hole out of the side of the carton between the notches. The soundbox hole can be round, square or in any shape the children design. Make a bridge to support the strings by cutting out and folding back a tab on either side of the soundhole. String the rubber bands through the notches and you have a ukulele.

Tambourines   For each tambourine you need four bottle caps, a one-by-one-by-six-inch block of wood, two small nails and one larger nail. Use the larger nail to put holes in the center of the bottle caps. Nail two bottle caps onto the block of wood with each smaller nail. Make sure that the bottle caps can shake freely.

Drums   Use oatmeal or grits containers with their original tops. You can also use coffee cans upside down, or cover the top of any can with canvas or other heavy fabric secured with rubber bands. Have children paint and decorate the drums.

Maracas   Put dried beans or gravel in a container and shake! Potato chip cans work well.

Xylophone   For each xylophone you need a stick or long piece of wood and nails in a range of sizes. Hammer the nails in the wood from smallest to largest. Use the largest nail to make music by striking the sides of the other nails. The range of sound is a result of the variety of nail sizes.

Sand Blocks   For each set of sand blocks, you need two two-by-four-inch blocks of wood and two sheets of sandpaper to cover the wood and glue. Glue the sandpaper to the wood blocks and let dry. For additional support, use thumbtacks on the sides of the wood. Rub together for a great scratchy sound.

Making Musical Instruments

13 Sometimes We Can All Win
Creative Conflict Resolution

New Responses

When we first go into a classroom and ask children "What would you do if someone hit you?" they often respond "I would hit 'em back." Children usually do not see any alternatives to violence. The Children's Creative Response to Conflict program (CCRC) makes possible new responses by helping children acquire an awareness of the complexities of conflict, explore alternatives in conflict situations and choose the most appropriate one to act upon.

As children learn to discover their own alternatives to conflict, they find the choice of alternatives ranges far beyond what they first thought possible. Creative response is limited only by the bounds of their own fertile imaginations.

The process of exploring responses to conflict teaches children through their real-life experience and helps them develop and clarify their own values, an essential step in creative conflict resolution. Through this process children realize that in the most effective solutions, everybody wins.

The CCRC program approaches conflict resolution with the following concepts in mind.

- –Conflict exists. It is not going away and we are not trying to do away with it. We want to teach the skills to deal with conflict.
- –Conflict can lead to growth. Conflict is not always good, but it is not always bad either. We can learn new things about ourselves and others. Through conflict we can grow.
- –There are many possible solutions to any conflict. We practice generating ideas.
- –How we define a conflict is related to how we resolve it. The more accurately we define a problem the more likely we are to solve it.
- –Not everyone will define a problem in the same way. Often our confusion over solving a problem is related to our different definitions of a problem.
- –Violence escalates. We see this over and over in conflicts.
- –Positive feelings escalate, too. The more we affirm others and ourselves, the easier it becomes, and the more affirmed we feel.
- –Sometimes we can find solutions in which everyone wins. Not always, but sometimes.

Techniques to Develop Solutions

All of the exercises in this book contribute to an atmosphere in which conflicts can be dealt with and resolved creatively. When children work together and practice communicating with and affirming each other, they develop mutual respect and a desire to solve problems together.

The exercises and techniques in this chapter enable children to deal with immediate classroom problems as well as to find solutions to conflicts they will encounter in real life.

Vicarious Experience

In the following activities children encounter and solve problems through vicarious experience. Some activities are more effective in small groups where children can more readily contribute to and discuss creative solutions. If you intend to use these activities, refer to chapter four on small groups, page 13. All of these activities use discussion to stimulate children to consider and evaluate the solutions they come up with. When children encounter a problem similar to one they have already resolved, they are better prepared to meet it with a creative solution.

Skits   Describe a conflict situation for the class to enact as a skit. Choose a conflict relevant to their experience; for instance, a younger sister takes a book from an older sister, and they fight over it until the mother comes into the room. What should she do? (For other examples, refer to chapter fourteen on conflict scenarios.)

Interrupt the skit before the conflict is resolved to allow children to suggest their own solutions. Children are less likely to generate many alternatives if a solution is presented in the skit, especially younger children who will imitate what they see. Form small groups to discuss the conflict and possible solutions. Have one child in each group act as facilitator and ask the following questions:

   –What was the conflict?
   –What is one solution you can think of?
   –Which solution should we try to enact as a group?
   –Which role do you want to play in the solution?

Have the groups choose solutions to work into skits and rehearse them. When the groups are ready have them perform their skits for the class. After presentations, summarize the various solutions and have children discuss them and their feelings during the skits. You can also have groups simply share their solutions for the purpose of discussion, but acting out the skits is fun for everyone, including teachers!

Puppetry   Young or shy children often find it easier to express themselves and their feelings through puppets. You can use puppets instead of skits to present a conflict to the class. Have children form small groups to discuss the conflict, decide on a solution and present it to the class using puppets. Afterward encourage children to discuss the various solutions presented.

Roleplaying

Roleplaying uses feedback to help children discover new ways to respond to conflict. In roleplaying, a child's conditioned responses may be directly challenged as they are found to be inappropriate or ineffective. This leads children to examine alternative solutions.

How to Do a Roleplay

Roleplaying is a good technique for finding solutions to conflict. Describe a conflict situation to the class, define the roles and ask for volunteers to do a roleplay. Be sure children completely understand the details of the conflict before beginning the roleplay. Let the roleplay come to a natural end through resolution of the conflict, or stop it when children begin to repeat themselves. Ask how the characters in the roleplay felt and have others share their observations. Instead of describing a conflict to the class, an alternative is to have children brainstorm situations they want to work on (see page 63) and choose one to roleplay.

Roleplaying can also be used to find solutions to immediate real-life conflicts. For example, if two children are fighting over a book bag which each thinks is his, ask them to stop and roleplay a different solution. One response may be that they look inside the bag. Roleplay the conflict again and discuss the various solutions. Role reversal (see the following section) can be particularly effective in solving immediate conflicts.

Some Special Techniques that Can Be Used in Roleplaying

The Freeze Technique can be used during a roleplay to stop the action and find out why the characters are acting as they are or how they are feeling about what is happening. You can ask them directly or ask a specific question, such as "What is one thing the other child said or did that you are reacting to?" By breaking down the conflict into individual actions, children can see how a conflict escalates or how a solution is prevented by an attitude, a small action, a failure to listen, etc. The freeze technique also helps children to see how a certain action can lead to a solution.

Role Reversal helps children look at both sides of a conflict. Often a conflict seems impossible to solve because children view each other as enemies and not persons. Role reversal enables children to understand each other's point of view by experiencing what the other is going through. After completing a roleplay, have the same children repeat it switching their roles. Ask children how they felt in their new roles and discuss any new solutions that developed. You can also ask, "Which of the solutions seemed real or preferable?" Role reversal can be used in small or large groups.

Alter Ego can be used with roleplaying to look at a conflict in more depth. Each character has someone standing next to him or her to act as an alter ego. The alter ego says what the character is really thinking as opposed to what he or she is saying in the roleplay.

Video Playback is an effective way to analyze a roleplay. Videotape an entire roleplay without interruption. Before playing it back, announce that children can stop the tape whenever they see something to question or comment on. This is a good way to look at body language and analyze why conflict occurs. Video playback can also be used with skits and communication games. Teachers find it interesting to experiment with the uses of video. For further suggestions see **Affirmation Video,** page 47.

Special Types of Roleplaying

Quick Decision Roleplaying helps children think on their feet and come up with solutions quickly. Have children pair off; some may choose to observe. Name two characters in a roleplay and have children choose roles. Describe a conflict scenario involving the two characters and tell children they have one minute to roleplay it. Afterward have children discuss how they felt in their roles and what solutions they came up with. Then repeat the process.

Extended Roleplaying is used to analyze a complicated problem involving groups of people. It lasts longer than a regular roleplay and involves more characters, several of whom represent one point of view. Extended roleplaying can be used by parents or teachers to understand and find solutions to problems in the school or community, or a situation involving more than one problem.

Choose a scenario involving groups and describe the conflict. Form groups representing those involved in the conflict, giving detailed information to each one about the history and their role in the conflict. You may arrange a meeting between two or more of the groups. Give children enough time to think about their roles and plan what they will say to others before starting the roleplay.

Other Conflict Resolution Activities

The following exercises help children look at, gather information about and solve problems. They demonstrate that children working together on a problem generate a greater variety of solutions than one child working alone. These exercises also build community as children work together on problems and develop a sense of cohesiveness. Many of these exercises can also be used in teacher support groups to overcome feelings of isolation and promote a sense of community and trust.

Brainstorming is a method of generating alternative solutions to a problem. It develops children's ability to produce many responses to a question. The key question in brainstorming is "How many?" The likelihood of finding a unique solution increases with the number of solutions produced.

Brainstorming is fun in itself but is effective only as part of a problem-solving process. Use brainstorming as a tool for gathering ideas about a given problem. State the problem and ask a question, such as "What would *you* do in this situation?" Then have the group put forth ideas *without discussing or criticizing them*. The atmosphere should be nonjudgmental, no matter how crazy the ideas seem, in order to elicit unusual thoughts which may turn out to be most effective. Create an atmosphere where ideas are only ideas and not necessarily reflections of children. Have someone record the ideas on the blackboard where they can be seen by everybody. After children have exhausted their suggestions, review the list. Group together and simplify the items, if appropriate. Discuss ideas which seem most relevant in further detail.

Brainstorming can be used to find solutions to problems, to define problems, to find out what problems children want to work on, to find causes of conflict or be integrated into the curriculum. Use it wherever it fits.

Quick Decision Making helps children to find solutions to problems in a short period of time. Present a problem to the class, then form pairs or small groups to come up with solutions which are mutually acceptable. Limit this process to about one minute. Repeat the process with different conflicts until children are able to find solutions quickly. Have the class discuss the solutions and how it feels to make decisions under pressure.

Personal Conflict Stories help children look at different types of conflict and see their similarities. Form small groups and ask each child to tell about a conflict he or she once had. Then ask the following questions:

–How can we put these conflicts into a story?
–What are some solutions to the conflicts?
–Can we tie all these conflicts and solutions together in one story?

Use a tape recorder to preserve the stories. Some children may need help putting the story in final form. Use the exercise to develop writing ability and have children work together transcribing and illustrating the stories. Put the completed stories and illustrations in book form and pass them around for others to read and enjoy.

Instead of creating a book, have children put together personal conflict stories to form skits or puppet shows. Be sure children are clear about what they want to express before performing them.

Reading Conflict Stories fits well into existing curricula. Choose a story that presents a conflict and read it to the class, stopping just before the conflict is resolved. Ask children to brainstorm solutions to the conflict (see **Brainstorming,** page 63). Discuss the conflict together or in small groups and ask children which solution they want to see happen. After the discussion, finish reading the story and discuss its resolution of the conflict. This is one way to show children that there are many alternatives in solving problems and there is no need to stay locked into the same old ways of dealing with them.

Fairy Tale Writing uses a form children love to find solutions to problems. Present a problem and have children work individually or in groups on fairy tales which include a solution they want to see happen in real life. "Once upon a time there was a boy who couldn't get along with his little sister because she kept taking all of his books. One day the little sister took his favorite book and he got so mad that he yelled at her and made her cry." This activity can be used as a creative writing assignment. Some children may need help writing their own fairy tales, and some may prefer using a tape recorder. Children may want to put their conflicts in the context of actual fairy tales (Cinderella, Little Red Riding Hood, etc.) or create their own symbolic characters. Fairy tales can also be acted out as they are read.

Utopian Picture Drawing is a problem-solving exercise in which children draw an ideal school, community, neighborhood, etc. This exercise helps them think about what problems exist and what possible solutions there are. Working in pairs or small groups children are encouraged to cooperate in deciding what their pictures look like, while children working individually may develop their own unique vision. Pictures can be shared and discussed with the class and exhibited for others to see.

The Utopia Gallery helps children to become more specific about changes they want to occur. Choose a topic such as school and ask children what changes they want to see in school. You can ask children to say one thing they want to see changed and then form small groups to discuss the changes further. Children in groups can combine the visions (keeping notes is helpful) and present them to the class for further discussion. To be more specific, ask children what changes they want to see made in one month, one year, etc.

Comic Strips are an unusual and enjoyable conflict resolution activity. The exercise works well in any group which has learned to write. Draw a few panels of a conflict situation: a boy is walking through the park with a basketball; someone walks up to him and says "Give me that basketball!" Have children continue the comic strip by filling in the remaining panels with a solution of their own, working in small groups or individually. For younger children, provide worksheets with the first two panels already filled in. Older children can create their own comics "from scratch." If children work in small groups, put the comic strips on large sheets that can be exhibited on the wall. Afterward have children discuss the various solutions they have come up with. Be sure to stress that drawing ability is not important and stick figures are acceptable.

Comic Books can be put together by combining individual comic strips showing conflicts which children have experienced or made up. Children love working on comic books and find this a fun activity for a writing assignment.

The Box Surprise Tell the class there is a surprise package for them and produce a large box from which emerge two children dressed and made-up to look like puppets. The box has a card attached which reads, "We are mechanical puppets. We come alive when we have conflicts to solve." Ask the class to think of conflicts and make sure the mechanical puppets understand what the conflicts are. If the puppets don't understand, they should stand lifeless until the conflict is clarified. Have the puppets suggest enough solutions to stimulate a later discussion. The puppets should maintain their puppet qualities until they leave the room, when they remove their makeup and costumes and return as themselves, perhaps apologizing for being late!

Follow with a discussion of the various conflicts and their solutions. The fantasy element of this exercise makes it especially good for young children. Use children who have shown skill in quick decision making to play the part of the puppets.

Goal Wish Problem Solving is an exercise adapted from *The Practice of Creativity* by George M. Prince (see bibliography). This exercise provides a structure for children to work on their problems within a supportive group. Often a problem implies an accusation or blame, but formulating the solution as a "fantasy" or "goal wish" emphasizes finding a nonjudgmental solution. Using "I wish" language encourages children to come up with solutions without accusing others or placing blame. Consider as an example the following problem: A child continually puts down others in class. Instead of placing blame for the problem and saying "The teacher should make her stop putting others down," a "goal wish" solution can be "I wish the child could find something she is good at and

Comic Strips

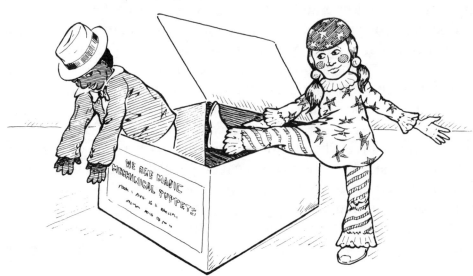

The Box Surprise

Conflict Video Tapes

feel better about herself." Limit the size of the groups to seven members. Groups should be homogeneous although people less familiar with problems discussed can often give a fresh, objective perspective. Each group selects a facilitator who also acts as recorder and follows these steps:

1. Brainstorm and record problems on the minds of children in the group (see **Brainstorming,** page 63). Give everyone an equal chance to contribute. Record problems where everyone can see them. Problems can be confined to one area, for instance, within a classroom.

2. Select a problem to deal with.

3. Have the "owner" of the problem take two or three minutes to describe it in detail so everyone understands it.

4. Brainstorm "fantasy" or "goal wish" solutions and record them.

5. Have the owner choose a solution from the list and identify any possible obstacles to it, and record them.

6. Have the group brainstorm and record ways to overcome the obstacles. Be sure at this point not to make the conflict larger.

7. Have the owner state how he or she will implement the solution and when he or she will start. Give the recorded solutions to the owner, and return to step 2. Have children proceed around the circle to facilitate equal participation, but allow children to pass and have a later opportunity.

This activity helps teachers to acquire a fresh outlook on persistent classroom problems.

The Card Game encourages children to share feelings about problems. Give each child a blank card and have them write down answers to a question, such as "What are three things you find difficult or annoying about school?" Shuffle the cards and pass them out so everyone has someone else's cards. Have children read one answer on the card and say how it relates to them. While this game does not develop solutions, it helps children realize that others share their worries and fears. The exercise builds community and offers ideas for skits and roleplays from the children's concerns.

Conflict Video Tapes use stories, skits or puppet shows children have already developed or made for the occasion. The object is for children to cooperate and create something which reflects everyone's input. Give everyone a say in choosing the conflicts and solutions to include in the tape and a role in producing the recording.

14

But How Do We Resolve the Problem?
Some Conflict Scenarios

This chapter is made up of examples of conflict familiar to children in school and elsewhere. They include conflicts between children, teachers and children, parents and children, and between adults. Use these examples to create your own scenarios, skits, puppet shows, roleplaying, discussions, brainstorming or problem solving. Many of the examples are good material for a discussion of how to mediate conflict. You can also discuss how humor sometimes helps to diffuse tensions.

Conflicts in School: Child-Child

While these conflicts are primarily between children, their solutions may involve a teacher.

Aggression   In the halls, a child knocks the books out of another child's arms, then steps on the books and laughs.

Exclusion   Two children are playing a game of catch or handball. A third child comes along and asks to play. One says "no" because she doesn't like the third child, and the other hesitates.

Putdown   One child wears old clothes to school. Another child puts him down consistently about his clothing.

Possession   Two children are fighting over a pencil. One accuses the other of stealing the pencil. The accused says she brought the pencil from home.

Teasing   In the cafeteria one child returns to his plate to find that someone has poured milk on his hot dog roll. There are at least two other children nearby.

Friends   In the cafeteria one child has two pieces of cake. She is eating one and gives the other to her best friend. A third child comes along and asks for some. The first child doesn't like the third child but her friend does.

Conflicts in School: Child-Teacher

Stealing   Money has been stolen from the teacher's desk. One child is suspected but there is no evidence.

Favoritism   Three children approach the teacher saying they think the teacher is playing favorites with another child, and they are sick of it.

Cheating   Two children are playing checkers during free time. One goes to the teacher and accuses the other of cheating.

Place in Line   Several children returning from gym are lined up at the drinking fountain. The teacher asks the second in line to get a paper from his desk. Afterward, the child wants to get back in his place in line.

Late Student   For the third day in a row, a child comes to class ten minutes late. The teacher has just finished giving directions to everyone else.

Unprepared Student   Halfway through directions for the lesson, the teacher notices that one child is not writing anything. The teacher discovers that the child does not have a pencil. This has happened several times before.

Cheating   The teacher suspects two children of cheating because of similar answers on a test. After finding an answer sheet in one of their desks, the teacher asks to talk with them after class.

Refusal to Follow Directions   The teacher asks a child to close the door. The student says no in a loud voice.

Fire Drill   School rules forbid talking during fire drills. One child sees water on the floor and warns the others. The teacher hears the child talking and asks her to stay after school.

Teacher Is Annoyed by Student   One child keeps raising his hand while the teacher is giving homework directions. The teacher has said to save all questions until the directions are finished, but the child keeps raising his hand because he is unable to hear.

Conflicts at Home: Sibling Rivalry

One Book for Two Children   Two children are at home one evening. One child is reading a comic book. The other child enters the room and wants to read the same comic book.

Whose Book?   At home a child is looking at a book her older sister checked out from the library. The older sister comes in and demands the book, saying it is hers. The younger one protests, saying she found it. The older sister says the younger one can't read anyway, but the younger one still wants the book.

Who Gets to Wear It?   Two brothers are getting dressed before school. One puts on a sweater that the other was going to wear that day. The first one says he was told he could wear it.

Conflicts at Home: Parent-Child

The following conflicts occur in the home and can be used as exercises by parent support groups or groups of parents and children working together.

Baby-sitting A twelve-year-old wants to take on a baby-sitting job to supplement his allowance. The job is for two or three afternoons a week. His parents do not know the family.

Responsibility A child comes home after playing with friends in time for dinner, unsuspecting that anything is wrong. The mother is furious because she told the child to come straight home after school to baby-sit while the mother went to a doctor's appointment.

Family Meeting A family is trying to figure out how to get the weekly chores done equitably and promptly. The mother used to do the chores herself but became frustrated and angry because no one helped her and she does not like asking for help continually.

Privacy A parent has found cigarettes in a child's pocket while doing the laundry. The parent does not approve of smoking and is upset that the child is being secretive. The child has just come home from school.

Children's Conflicts outside of School and Home

The following conflicts take place where there is no teacher or parent to help find a solution, though adults may be introduced for the purpose if so desired. These examples can be used with parents, teachers or after-school groups.

Moral Dilemma One child's father has told her never to climb trees again because he is afraid she will get hurt. She has promised not to climb trees anymore though she is very good at climbing and loves it. On the way to school she and a friend see a kitten caught in a tree. They are afraid the kitten will fall and her friend has never climbed a tree. Though she knows how to get the cat down, she remembers her promise to her father.

False Accusations In a store a child is browsing through comic books for one to buy. The child has read most of each series and is looking for a new issue. The vendor thinks the child is reading without paying or is getting ready to steal a book, and starts to yell at the child.

Problems with Bigger Kids (1)A child is playing with a new toy. A bigger child comes along and tries to take the toy away. (2)On the way to school a bigger child tries to take a younger one's lunch money.

Stealing Outside a store after school one child plots to steal cigarettes but he needs an accomplice since he was almost caught last time. The other child is reluctant to participate and feels it is not right.

Adult Conflict

Because creative conflict resolution is applicable to many situations, we include a few examples relevant to adults. The following can be used in faculty workshops, parent support groups, high school groups or elsewhere.

Stereo   You and your friend are listening to a record on the stereo. Your roommate wants to study.

Neighbors   There is an apple tree on the property line between your house and your neighbor's. You want it for your children to climb and you don't want spray on the tree, while your neighbor wants to prune it and harvest the apples. You both are trying to settle the problem to each other's satisfaction.

Subway   (1) One evening on the subway you notice a man staring at you. You move to another car, and he follows you. You get off at the next station, and so does he. The train is about to leave the platform. (2) On the subway, you see four teenage boys bothering someone on the train.

Street Hassle   (1) You are a woman walking home alone in the evening. A man walking along from the other direction bumps into you seemingly unintentionally and makes a nasty comment. (2) You are walking home alone in the evening when you notice two men close behind you. You cross the street, and so do they.

Theater   You have been waiting in front of a theater for a friend who invited you to a show and has the tickets. Your friend was supposed to meet you half an hour ago and it is now five minutes into the show. Your friend arrives but you can't go in until the intermission.

Mugging   You are walking along the street and someone comes up to you and demands your money. He is much bigger than you and says he has a knife although you do not see it.

15

Doesn't Anybody Understand?
The Need to Share Feelings and Develop Trust

Set aside a time in every activity for children to share feelings. It's important for children to discuss not only what they learned from an exercise, but also how it affected them. For example, a roleplay may elicit many feelings from a child's past. Sharing feelings brings children together and develops an atmosphere of trust and openness. In such an atmosphere children develop a conscious approach to affirmation, cooperation, communication and creative conflict resolution. To reach these goals it is important for children to be able to share both positive and negative feelings. The following exercises help children share their feelings and reach these goals.

The Sharing Circle promotes equal participation and a positive atmosphere. There are two ground rules: (1) Everyone has a chance to speak, and (2) Everyone is heard. Ask a question that will lead to an interesting discussion, such as "What would be in your ideal room?" Have children volunteer or go around the circle in turn, but limit each child's time to about thirty seconds. Use this exercise regularly and combine it with other techniques to improve the atmosphere in a group. Use it when conflicts arise to discuss problems in the class or integrate it into discussions of books, readings, plays, class trips or movies. As children become familiar with the *Sharing Circle* you can use it with more difficult topics, such as "Can you think of a time when you felt excluded?" Introduce such a topic only when children are comfortable with each other and with sharing feelings. Other topics for *Sharing Circles* include earliest memories, an enjoyable learning experience and an ideal family. *Sharing Circles* can go anywhere you want them to go and can be used with all ages, including parent and teacher support groups.

Social Barometer is a fun way for children to share feelings. Draw a number scale on the blackboard, ranging from plus five to minus five. Have children gather at the zero mark. Have someone call out questions to the group on topics such as movies, siblings, money, bicycles, going to the park, doing math, doing homework, cleaning your room, doing the dishes and sweeping the floor. Put questions in simple yes-or-no format, such as "Do you like to go to the movies?" or "Do you like the idea of having brothers or sisters?" Children with positive feelings about the question move toward that end of the scale, how far depending on how positive they feel. If they have negative feelings, they move toward the opposite end. If the entire class is too large to participate use small groups.

Trust Games help children feel positive about each other and develop a mood of cooperation. Use these games when children are comfortable sharing feelings and with each other.

The Blindfold Trust Walk teaches children to trust each other. Have children pair up. One child leads the other around blindfolded, explaining where they are going, what to expect and how to avoid falling or bumping into things. The blindfolded child should have complete trust in the leader. Have the partners switch roles. Afterward have children discuss how it felt to lead and be led. Children's reactions to trusting and being trusted often surprise them.

The Trust Fall builds community and is also affirming. Have children stand close together in a circle and hold out their hands. One child stands inside the circle and, keeping his or her body rigid, falls into the circle. Children in the path of the falling child catch the child and pass him or her around the circle. If there is time, allow everyone to have a turn.

The Trust Lift is similar to the *Trust Fall*. Begin with one child lying on the floor, face up. Have several children gather around the child and together lift the person. The one being lifted can be raised, lowered, or otherwise moved around, whenever the person being lifted or the group wants, and then lowered back down. In the *Trust Fall* as well as the *Trust Lift,* discuss how children in both roles felt during the exercise.

Masks Children Wear leads to a discussion of what roles are and when they are used. Begin with a brainstorming of situations children face in school or at home. This can include waking up, eating breakfast, riding the subway, forgetting homework, being in the cafeteria, having recess, getting teased, getting home late and eating dinner. Have children form small groups and make up skits involving situations from the brainstorming. When they have a clear idea of the situations and characters, have children create masks to show how they feel in response to each situation. For example, a child in the subway may wear a mask to express anger or loneliness. Another child who hands in homework late may wear a mask to express fear. Have children perform their skits and discuss them. Younger children have difficulty understanding the concept of roles but have an easy time "making faces."

Exclusion Exercises help children examine feelings of being excluded and excluding others. These are very delicate issues for children, and the activities should take place in an atmosphere of affirmation. One way to look at the theme of exclusion is to do a roleplay in which someone is excluded and discuss how children felt watching or being in the roleplay. The following exercises are other ways to look at exclusion.

The Gibberish Game helps children to think about their exclusion of others and to realize that others fear exclusion too. Have someone make nonsense sounds or talk gibberish in front of the class. Then have children turn to partners to practice gibberish. Next, form groups of three and ask children to talk gibberish to each other. Have children exclude one member of the group by leaving him or her out of the gibberish and directing it only toward the other person. Repeat this three times so everyone in the group has a chance to be excluded. Afterward have the class discuss how it felt to exclude and to be excluded. Do the *Gibberish Game* quickly so children are excluded only for a moment. Occasionally children are bothered about being excluded, but most accept the game as a way to analyze the issue. Anyone who feels bad about being excluded should be affirmed.

The Physical Exclusion Game also helps children analyze how they feel excluding or being excluded. Begin by having children form a tight circle, wrapping their arms together. One child is outside of the circle and tries to get in. When that child gets in, another one leaves the circle and tries to get in. Give as many children as time allows a chance to try to get into the circle. If someone is unable to get in, he or she should be excluded for no more than a minute or so. Let the child into the circle and ask another one to try to break in. Afterwards, discuss the different ways to get into the circle and how the exercise felt to the children.

16 How Did It Work?
Let's Evaluate

Evaluation is a time set aside in an activity to encourage feedback. It can be done at the end of an activity, during an activity, or both. Evaluation shows children that an activity is for them and their input is valued. Encourage evaluation and incorporate the feedback into planning for new activities. Evaluation is affirming and group building, and helps both teachers and children to learn from experience.

Thumbs Up, Hands Out, Thumbs Down is an exciting and quick way to evaluate a succession of activities. It indicates whether or not children like an activity; not how or why. One at a time, name activities the group has recently completed. If children liked an activity, they put their thumbs up. If it was just okay, they put their hands out extended. If they disliked it, they put their thumbs down. Some children at first may put thumbs down or up just for the fun of it. But if you take it seriously, eventually they will see it as an important way to communicate their likes and dislikes. If there is unanimous disapproval of an activity, take the time to ask children why they didn't like it.

One-to-One Interviewing is a more in-depth form of evaluation than *Thumbs Up*. Interview children privately, asking specific questions concerning the activities you did. Conducting interviews after the first few activities can aid you in planning for the year. If you want to document the evaluation, tape record it; children love to use the tape recorder.

Verbal Evaluation after each activity allows you to gather immediate feedback. Verbal feedback is valuable because it can be translated readily into new and improved activities. You can ask, "What is one thing you liked about today's session? What is one thing you want to see changed? What is one thing you didn't like? What is one thing you want to see happen in the future?" Direct questions are helpful in making up a new plan.

An Evaluation Sheet indicates those activities children liked most and least. List in one column all the activities the class has done. To the right put three columns, one headed by a smiling face to indicate approval of an activity; one headed by a neutral face to indicate indifference and one headed by a frowning face, to indicate disapproval. You can also include questions, such as "What activity did you like the best? What do you want to see added? What is one thing you never want to do again?" Or have children put a star beside activities they liked best. Use the evaluation sheet after several activities have been completed. For further information on evaluation, see chapters three and four, especially page 12.

ACTIVITIES
What did you think of them?

Things We Did (these items change for each workshop session evaluation)	🙂	😐	☹️
Writing one positive thing about each person in class			
Small group sharing circles			
Interviewing			
Making the Affirmation Notebooks			
Skits			
Building machines in small groups			
Pantomime this object			
Zoom			
What did you like best?			

17 Why Only in Classrooms?
Expanding Our Skills to Meet Wider Needs

Although most of our work has been with elementary school children and teachers, we have done many workshops with younger and older children, family groups and groups with mixed age ranges. We have also been in contact with people who have used our ideas working with other groups. We hope these examples stimulate your thinking about how to use these activities with your group.

Younger Children

With younger children (kindergarten and preschool) use the shorter and more active games which hold their attention. Young children love ritual and rhythm games and songs. Use puppets to get shy children to talk. Puppetry is an easier conflict resolution tool for them than roleplaying or skit making. Activities using symbolism and analysis are difficult, while affirmation and cooperation games are usually very successful. Specific exercises which work well are *Community Music Making, Machine Building, Pantomime This Object, Rainstorm, Herman-Hermina, Human Protractor, Touch Blue, Zoom, My Bonnie* and most of the loosening-up exercises (which we call "copycat games" with younger children).

Many of the other exercises can be adapted for young children. For example, a variation on *Grab Bag Dramatics* for children unable to put together plays is to pass the grab bag around and have each child pantomime something with the object s/he took from the bag.

High School Students

Many of the exercises and techniques were originally used with high school students and adults before they were adapted for elementary school children. Others need only a simple change of content to be appropriate. For example, in the *Memory Name Game*, instead of asking players what their favorite dessert is, ask them to name their favorite sport or one thing they enjoy doing on a Saturday morning.

High school teachers concerned with the integration of these ideas into the curriculum will find many exercises adaptable to their needs. *Goal Wish Problem*

Solving can be used to analyze a historical event. The *Affirmation Notebook* can be turned into a creative writing project to stress positive experiences and relationships. Have science students cooperatively construct a classification system for vertebrates. High school teachers may use conflict resolution or problem-solving techniques such as roleplaying or skit making to deal with actual conflicts or to better understand historical conflicts. *Elephant and Palm Tree* can be adapted to the construction of geometric figures.

Emotionally Disturbed Children

Although we have had little direct experience in this area, we have learned of the success others have had using CCRC ideas with emotionally disturbed children. The following letter, describing experiences with an earlier edition of this book, comes from Emily Whiteside, Supervisor of Clinical Services at the Developmental Evaluation Center in Wilmington, North Carolina:

> I had a most exciting year using the *Handbook* with a class of nine mentally retarded children in a special education class in Wilmington, North Carolina. The children's ages ranged from seven to ten and this was a class in a public school setting. As the most significant presenting problem was inappropriate social skills among the children, the teacher and I focused upon developing positive relationships. The children chose the name of Super Friends for their special group and we met once a week for 45-minute sessions from January to May of 1975.
>
> Programs exploring the meaning of friendship were provided for self-learning, which resulted in the increase of the children's self-confidence. It was observed that even at such an early age, the children's identity had already been affected by being identified by others as "retarded." The group setting which viewed "self" in a "new light" allowed new self-images to unfold of being worthy individuals.
>
> The use of creative channels of learning which explored the imaginative feeling life such as puppets, fairy tales and roleplay of life situations were used. This seemed to be an ideal way to let children teach themselves, who have lowered intellectual functioning. The *Handbook* provided excellent suggestions and served as a guide to help the children with work on conflict resolution. Roleplay was the main technique used. It gave the children the opportunity to discuss their feelings and to observe desired behavior patterns while teaching them to discriminate between appropriate and inappropriate behavior patterns.
>
> As working with children is a most delicate process of an organic nature . . . time must pass before fruit matures. The teacher and I viewed our task somewhat as planting seeds that might nourish the flowering of these children's own self as it found greater expression through an appreciation of others. The dawn of the harvest has already begun in one child's experiences. Several weeks ago upon making a school visit to a child who had been transferred to a new school, the teacher observed significant progress. A depressed child who had formerly been expelled from school for two weeks because of his aggressive behavior was reported to be cooperative with others, to have a positive attitude toward school, was performing well academically and most important, to be happy within himself. Thus, one can know that the patient and caring attitude of others toward a child has a catching quality that grows and grows.

Teacher Workshops

Educators may develop teacher workshops with any of the following goals:

–To share ideas on new techniques.

–To find ways to incorporate new techniques into daily classroom life.

–To develop a support group for teachers to work together and solve problems creatively.

Each group of teachers is different. Some may want the help of an outside facilitator. Others may want to choose facilitators from among themselves. Our experience indicates that several elements contribute to a successful workshop:

–Make the administration aware of the project. Ask for the administration's support and, if possible, for special time for teachers to meet.

–Seek members who actively desire to participate, rather than take part because others want them to or they feel pressured.

–Make the emphasis of the group clear from the beginning. Some teachers may want to work on problem solving for actual classroom situations. Others may prefer to learn and try them out in the classroom. Others may want simply to share ideas.

–Promote a healthy group dynamic so members feel good about each other. Encourage equal sharing, mutual support, openness and willingness to work out conflicts.

–Make the process of the workshop more important than the product. Discuss each activity after it is done, adapting it to your situation.

–Create an open atmosphere to encourage creative thinking and new ideas. A good example of such possibilities is the *Imaginary World* (see page 28).

One group that used teacher workshops was the Park Slope Day Care Center, which operates units in fifty homes with children ages three to twelve. As they explain:

> Initially the group was directed in exercises that developed trust and affirmation. Slowly but perceptibly, communication was developed and a cooperative spirit spread through the group. The concepts behind conflict resolution were presented by solving actual misunderstandings in the group. Individuals were given the opportunity to act out feeling and nonsense ideas (nonsense ideas that held the key to unlocking deeper feelings). Staff members actually used the techniques on each other that they would employ with children, and they saw that these methods are effective for lessening adult tensions and conflicts as well. The growth of the staff's understanding which was brought about by the careful leadership of trainer Lenny Burger led to increased harmony, if not actual peace.
>
> Beyond the group, training and techniques learned from it were brought to bear on individual cases both in the center and in the homes where children are cared for.

One of the most interesting series of teacher workshops we have facilitated was a course at the City College of New York's Department of Elementary Education. Particularly innovative in this course was the integration of our participatory approach with Piaget's observations on the moral development of children. Teachers using this book and particularly those interested in teacher workshops may read accounts of the course in the appendix.

Alternatives to Violence Project: Prison and Community Workshops

Children's Creative Response to Conflict was initiated in 1972 by the Quaker Project on Community Conflict (QPCC). Three years later QPCC's founder, Lawrence Apsey, initiated the Alternatives to Violence Project (AVP) at Green Haven, a maximum-security prison in New York State. Although AVP's main focus is on prison workshops, there has been a growing demand for its services from community groups such as service organizations, shelters for battered women and the homeless, programs for violence-prone youth, church groups and probation officers.

Using the four themes of cooperation, affirmation, communication and conflict resolution, the success of AVP indicates how applicable these concepts are for all ages and environments. A number of our facilitators also conduct workshops for AVP, which we consider a sister program to our own. To convey the success of the AVP approach, we reproduce here an article from the *Staten Island Advance* of November 25, 1986 on the AVP program at Arthur Kill Prison on Staten Island.

Prisoners Learn That There Are Alternatives to Violent Behavior

by Beth Jackendoff
Advance Staff Writer

Eight men—among them arsonists, armed robbers and murderers—sit in a circle. One man stands in the center. After a moment's reflection, he says, "A big wind blows on—*everyone wearing green!*"

The room explodes with laughter. All of them are wearing green in the form of drab prison-issue pants, because all of them are inmates at Arthur Kill Correctional Facility. Within seconds, each one has jumped up and taken another seat, leaving a different man standing.

No, it's not musical chairs for prisoners. This exercise—light-hearted as it may seem—is actually part of the Alternatives to Violence Project, an experience that has transformed the lives of 6,000 inmates around the state.

AVP started in 1975 in Green Haven, a maximum security jail near Poughkeepsie, N.Y. A group of inmates there—almost all of them sentenced to life imprisonment for murder—asked to be taught the conflict resolution and non-violence techniques practiced by the Religious Society of Friends, commonly known as Quakers.

"That was such a successful program that when the inmates were transferred to other institutions they said, 'We've got to get this program here,' " said Lee Stern, a coordinator of AVP for many years and one of the program's founders.

Today there are waiting lists for AVP workshops at prisons all over the state. At Arthur Kill, prisoners must wait six months to participate in the program, because of a shortage of outside volunteers needed to run AVP. Currently outside facilitator Carmel Kussman runs the AVP workshops at Arthur Kill with the help of a few inmates who have been involved with the program for several years. (For more information on how to volunteer for AVP, call the Religious Society of Friends at 212 477-1067.)

The AVP workshops consist of nine sessions given over three full days and evenings. Many of the exercises teach the prisoners how to deal with frustrating real-life situations. In one role-play, an ex-convict tries to convince an employer to hire him. In another, a just-released inmate learns to get along with his wife, who has become used to life without him.

Another scenario concerns avoiding the "crimeys," i.e., the cohorts from the inmate's past who may be waiting to bring him back into the ne'er-do-well gang.

"If you run with these guys, you can wind up back in here crippled or be in here for life," said Michael, an inmate at Arthur Kill who has helped run nearly 50 AVP workshops since he first heard about the program in 1980. "It's just a matter of time—the police know you have a record. With AVP, you're looking at alternatives to that. You can say, hey, there's more to life."

In one AVP exercise designed to teach cooperation, a small group takes five minutes to decide what to build with a set of toy blocks. They then have to work in absolute silence to create their structure. There are also light-hearted tension-breakers, such as the "Big wind blows on so-and-so" exercise described above.

But the most fundamental aspect of the program is its emphasis on self-confidence and learning to trust. Michael started a recent workshop by saying, "In the next three days, what we're going to develop is what you rarely see in a prison situation: a family. A lot of barriers will break down. We've been taught from day one to put others down, but here, we look for the good in everyone and we're reaffirming the good."

One of the participants in the session picked up on that theme. "Everybody here, we all come in here, nervous, tense, saying 'How's he looking at me'" he said. "But here we say, what's the positive way? You find out what makes this person tick, rather than getting in a beef with a guy and hitting him in the face.

Basically our goal is to become like a family, to show concern, rather than just go off the deep blue."

Prisoners say that the friends they make through AVP help them learn to believe in themselves. "I needed a change in my life," explained Mac, an inmate and AVP trainer. "I used to be a violent person, but the people there, the support, the help they gave me, helped me change. They showed love to me. They was there for me. It just turned me around. This is the right direction for me."

Although Mac is soon to be let out of jail on parole, prison officials say that AVP experience is not a ticket to early release. Indeed, parole has been denied to several of the inmates who are most active in the program.

"Three of us in here—all trainers—are living proof that it's not going to convince the parole board to let you go home," said inmate and AVP trainer Hank Heinsohn. "But none of us have quit the program because of that. In fact, once you get beyond the point of doing it for the parole board, you get a lot more out of it."

The trainers also recognize that not every prisoner who signs up for the program will be able to change his behavior. "But the importance of the program is to plant those seeds and teach people to learn to think about putting them into practice," said Rich, another AVP trainer incarcerated at Arthur Kill.

Michael agreed, "Alternatives to Violence means being able to say, I've been ruled by my emotions. I may not be able to control every one of them. But what are my alternatives and how do I find them? It starts from within."

Most of the AVP techniques for avoiding confrontations are simply a matter of mind over might. When you find yourself in a conflict with someone, said Rich, "you say something nice instead of perpetuating the argument. Think about the other guy as a human being. And you do it not out of weakness, but out of inner strength and belief."

"Sometimes it means having to walk away from a situation," said Michael. "Sometimes it means having to take a lot of grub. But if my taking a little crap from you now might change your life, that's OK. I have enough control that I'm not going to get into a situation where either of us is killed."

Hank put it this way: "Lots of people around here suffer from the James Cagney or

John Wayne syndrome. They feel that tough-guy image has to be maintained. It's the little pesty stuff that gets them in trouble. A lot of violence is perpetrated over televisions and washing machines. Basically what we're trying to do is bring a non-violent solution to the conflicts. If you don't let your feelings be known, then you're going to start building up a resentment. Do not let yourself fall into traps like that. Instead, communicate."

AVP participants range from small-time swindlers to convicted murderers. But in-

terestingly, many of the trainers—those most committed to AVP—are in for violent crimes, often homicide. Perhaps working in AVP, said Rich, is "a way of giving atonement, of giving something back to society." Or maybe it's a matter of insight. "If you're in for a violent offense, you know what happened and why it happened," said Michael.

But the message of AVP is the same for all participants, whatever their crimes. As one inmate put it, "A man who gets physical is a man who ran out of ideas."

Alternatives to Violence Project

Outline of Typical Three-Day Seminar

Book: *Transforming Power for Peace*
Leaflets: *Introduction to Transforming Power* and *Guidelines for the Use of Transforming Power*
Nine sessions—2½ hours each

Session 1
Opening talk
Agenda review with names of team
Introduce team
Introduce everyone: Go around circle with name and one thing I hope to get out of this workshop
Adjective name exercise
Affirmation, in twos
Light-and-lively: *Big Wind Blows*
Brainstorm and discussion: What is violence?
Evaluation and closing

Session 2
Gathering: Name a favorite food
Agenda review
Concentric circles
Light-and-lively name games: *Name Frisbee, Yarn Name Game, 1-2-3-4-5 Name*, etc.
Sharing: A conflict I solved nonviolently
Listening exercise
Evaluation and closing

Session 3
Gathering: A sport I really enjoy
Agenda review

Transforming power rap
Light-and-lively
Power 1-2-3-4
Evaluation
Closing: Texas hug

Session 4
Agenda review
Gathering: What transforming power means to me
Principles of transforming power
Light-and-lively: *Owl and Mouse*
Broken Squares
Tinkertoy construction
Evaluation and closing

Session 5
Agenda review
Gathering: I feel good about myself when ...
Introduction to roleplays
Roleplays (in small groups, with video if wanted, interspersed with light-and-livelies as needed)
Evaluation and closing

Session 6
Agenda review
Gathering: A hiding place I had as a child

Empathy
Light-and-lively
More roleplays
Trust Circle and/or *Trust Lift*

Session 7
Agenda review
Gathering
Recap: Learnings from roleplays
A cooperative planning and action exercise
    (*Building a New Society, Coalition Exercise, Strategy Exercise*)
Light-and-lively
Who Am I?
Evaluation and closing

Session 8
This session is left free to accommodate any additional exercises that seem needed in this particular group.

Session 9
Agenda review
Gathering
Reflection exercise
Discussion: Where do we go from here? and unanswered questions
Affirmation Posters or *Affirmation Shields*
Evaluation of entire workshop
Graduation
Closing circle

Appendix

When the Children's Creative Response to Conflict program began, we spent much of our time doing workshops in classrooms with children and their teachers. We often went as a team of three, four or even five facilitators. We frequently had volunteers and students working with us. Marge Rice, one volunteer, expresses her feelings about her CCRC experience in the following poem. It not only captures the spirit of our early work with children, but also reflects what we did in those pilot years. The class reviews and the accounts of the course we taught at City College which follow give a sense of our subsequent development.

Kaleidoscope

The never-ending variety of creative
   solutions from:
THE KIDS . . .
THE CREATIVE KIDS.

Coming up out of the subway:
New York City!
Breakfast together at George's restaurant;
then,
The smoke-filled teacher's room at 75.
Pris's guitar,
Marge's camera.

Waiting in the hall outside the classroom:
"Are they ready for us yet?"
As we enter . . .
The joyous round of
Applause
that always greets
Lenny, Gretchen, and Pris . . .
The boys:
"Lenny, sit by me!"
"Sit here, sit here!"

Pris: "Shall we start with a song?"
Their very-most favorite:
"One bottle of pop, two bottles of pop . . ."

Gretchen: "Does anyone have a suggestion
for a conflict
they'd like to see roleplayed today?"
"Yeh, I do:
my little sister
is always getting into my things . . ."

"Me too:
on my vacation,
I went into a gift shop
and the man wouldn't wait on me
because I'm Jewish . . ."

The never-ending variety
of creative solutions
from
THE KIDS! . . .
THE CREATIVE KIDS!

"What is teasing?
Can you remember a time
when you were teased? . . .
How did it feel? . . ."

The never-ending variety
of creative solutions
from
THE CREATIVE KIDS!

Room building . . .
Machine building,
Monster drawings . . .
Silhouettes.

At the end,
"Shall we close with a song?"
Then,
before we leave,
moving all the desks
back in place.

Meeting back at Gretchen's apartment . . .
"What was your reaction
to the session as a whole? . . ."
"How was the teacher involvement
   today . . ."
"Next time
shall we try conflict resolution
with sock puppets?"

Lunchtime
back at the school:
Evaluation with the teacher:

"How can I break up
the cliques
in this classroom? . . ."
Genuine concern.
Real searching.
Openness.

Getting to know David, the student teacher
The Manhattan College
Peace Studies interns . . .
Ever-widening circles
of resources,
and support.

Overheard,
at the end of a session:
"Boy, I felt tired when I came to school
    today,
but now
I feel great!"
How to make the day
for a Project trainer.

Class Reviews

Workshop Experiences

The following class reviews reflect the growth of the Children's Creative Response to Conflict program. The first year's work focused primarily on conflict resolution as shown by the first review. The second year we developed communication skills, working with a teacher to improve her students' listening, speaking and observation abilities. The third review reflects our work on the theme of affirmation which continues to be an important part of the program. By the third year, we had thus established the program's themes of cooperation, communication, affirmation and conflict resolution.

In the fourth year, we became concerned with finding ways to integrate our program into the classroom and curriculum. The fourth review reflects our approach of addressing children's cognitive and affective development together. While we had conducted teacher workshops for several years, they became a central concern during the 1976–77 school year. The fifth review highlights a series of in-service teacher workshops for the Montclair, New Jersey schools. While our priority continues to be working with children in at least one school, we are increasingly involved with providing workshops for teachers.

1. A Fifth and Sixth Grade Class on the Upper West Side, New York City

This public school was situated in an integrated and gentrified neighborhood in Manhattan. The student population was approximately one-third black, one-third Latino and one-third white. The school had been conducting an experimental "open corridor" program in half of its classrooms and had bilingual classes and other programs run by outside resource people.

Marty Burke taught a successful open classroom where the children held daily meetings. The sixth graders (half of the class) were familiar with CCRC workshops from the year before, and the teacher considered our program one of his priorities. The children accepted us from the beginning, and therefore we never had any major attention or discipline problems. These children had had several years of experience in the open corridor program choosing activities and structuring their free time. The class was divided into well-defined areas that allowed several activities to take place simultaneously. Therefore our sessions could take place in one area while children who chose to work on other projects were free to do so. This structure was compatible with our philosophy of voluntary participation and was a major element of our success.

We began our program using a variety of formats, since we were developing our program as we went along. First we used puppetry to create a playful environment and relax the children. We then enacted a simple brother-sister conflict and used small groups to discuss solutions. This introduction to conflict resolution led the children to deduce that we were there to explore "learning about people."

Next we introduced the concept of roles to show the violence intrinsic to certain roles people play. We demonstrated the concept with a skit about a character who goes through the day confronting different situations and dealing with each one by wearing a different mask. After the skit, children listed the masks they saw themselves wearing. Using their lists, children found it easy to talk about themselves and the roles they played. Children created their first skits and, using their masks, were less inhibited about being in front of the class. The skits led to discussions about the ways people protect themselves and how roles vary with changing situations.

We then moved on to roleplaying as a technique to find solutions to conflicts. Children found it easier to use roleplaying in conjunction with skits rather than puppet shows. When they saw workshop facilitators roleplaying, children were eager to try it. Marty also practiced roleplaying with them during the rest of the week, which helped them pick up this tool more quickly.

We developed a format of opening our workshops with a skit, discussing it and roleplaying solutions to the problem presented. Toward the end of the year, we stopped using skits altogether and instead roleplayed solutions to conflicts suggested by the children.

Discussions in the beginning were general and unfocused because of our nondirectiveness and the children's eagerness to tell anecdotes. We later chose more specific goals for each session and began to focus discussions around one or two points. This increased the momentum and children's participation in the workshops. Because of our success with large group discussions, we favored this format and ceased experimenting with small groups.

We began theme development with the topics of bullies and street violence and moved to more personal themes such as conflict in the family and classroom. We encouraged children's participation every week by asking "What could you do to improve the situation?" Children roleplayed solutions to test their ideas. Gradually our approach produced new responses including being persistent, taking initiative, asking for help, becoming a mediator, waiting quietly until the appropriate moment, speaking calmly, bargaining, compromising and using humor to diffuse negative energy.

Children's trust grew as they began to discuss their feelings and discover that others in the class shared them. Children reported in personal interviews that our sessions were important to them because "they help us learn how to solve our problems." They began to note conflicts they saw and kept a list of them in the classroom. Each week we used the list in planning the next session, which helped them become more self-directed.

Children brought us problems to work on, and once we built an entire session around a conflict in process as we entered the room. We focused the session on one child and her relationship to her classmates. We used an affirmation exercise with much success, but decided afterward to generalize future problems in order to increase participation. Children especially enjoyed the affirmation and validation exercises, and having roleplays and discussions supplemented by other exercises and games.

Several parents who visited our sessions wanted to know more about our program. With their help we held a presentation for parents to show videotapes of our work in the classroom. Parents discussed changes they had observed in their children and mentioned that some children had initiated family discussions with positive results. Their children demonstrated a new willingness to see the point of view of other family members. One parent said her son had made a schedule of house chores which eliminated the confusion over them. In general parents felt their children were learning to handle situations with new self-confidence.

We worked with this class for the entire year and held a total of thirty workshops. During this time we saw children develop the following qualities:

–Children showed consistent willingness to attend the workshops. We were able to attract and direct their attention with the outcome that children became open to the concept of creative response to conflict.

–Children were active participants in the workshops. They reacted with enjoyment and responded voluntarily in exercises and discussions. They began to seek creative solutions to their conflicts and showed satisfaction with the sessions by thanking us each week.

–Children attached great worth to the sessions and desired to improve their skills in conflict resolution. Some of the values they adopted were expressed in their classroom behavior and in the feedback we received from parents and the teacher. Their ability to work together as a group to solve problems was consistent and stable.

2. A Fourth Grade Class in East Harlem, New York City

This school, located in a mixed black and Puerto Rican neighborhood which had experienced some violent episodes, had a warm, friendly atmosphere. Most of the classes were traditional, supplemented by a few open classrooms. Some of the children lived in nearby shelters, and many of them needed more attention than they received. We were welcomed by the administrators, teachers and students every time we visited the school.

Pam Mulligan ran a traditional, well-disciplined class, exhibited good control and was consistent in handling discipline problems. She was honest with the children and cared deeply for them, which was revealed in the atmosphere of trust in the class.

We decided against a conflict resolution approach, feeling the children would benefit more from workshops on affirmation and community building. We found that children were able to meet in a large group successfully. Our first workshop focused on conflicts between siblings which the children appeared happy to discuss. Compared to other family problems, the children did not consider sibling rivalry a major difficulty. The goals of our first few sessions were to gain rapport with the children, familiarize them with the program and discover what issues they needed and wanted to work on. We did one session on the role of the teacher to show that a teacher is a human being. But without an understanding of roleplaying, it was difficult for the children to be objective and imagine themselves in the teacher's place. Later in the year when we did a similar session the children were better able to be objective and understand both sides of a situation.

We felt a need to work with the class on communication skills and so did ten workshops in this area. The workshops on listening skills included structured games such as *Telephone, Paraphrasing, Following Directions* and *Storytelling,* using a tape recorder to examine whether each part of the story was heard. The workshops on observation skills included *Magician, Open-Closed, Observation, Eyewitness Skit* and *Fishbowl.* We also did workshops on speaking skills using *Inquiring Reporter, Small Group Interviewing, Diaphragm Breathing, Distance Speaking* and *Speaking in Front of the Group.* Since the children had difficulty articulating their feelings through drawings, this technique was unsuccessful. (The above exercises are described in chapter nine.)

These workshops succeeded because most of the activities included everyone as either participant or observer. For example in *Small Group Interviewing,* one child was interviewed while others thought up questions to ask. A second reason these workshops succeeded was through the use of a make-believe world. *Magician, Storytelling* and *Observation* are good examples of this. Children resisted drawing pictures and making skits about school, but were enthusiastic when given topics such as "at the circus," "in the park" or "at McDonald's." Third, children liked challenging games and exercises as long as we explained them clearly. Often we demonstrated games to help children better understand them. We tried to show rather than describe activities verbally, because children were much more attentive to our actions than words.

We also learned it was important for the teacher to be involved in games and exercises. One time the teacher played a part in a skit that the children found amusing, which lowered the risk level and encouraged children to participate. When the teacher took us seriously, children found more validity in the workshops. From our point of view, it was important to have the teacher act as a facilitator as often as possible. Therefore we made an effort to communicate before, during and after our workshops. We called the teacher the night before the workshop to go over our plans and held an evaluation after each session.

After the workshops on communication skills, we were ready to work on conflict resolution. By then children had developed some skills in roleplaying and skits and felt comfortable sharing personal experiences. We chose street problems and exclusion as our themes. We did roleplays on children being robbed in the street and discussed ways to handle the problem. We also used exclusion games such as *Gibberish* and *Physical Exclusion.*

Singing did not work well in this class. Usually when we arrived to do a workshop, the children were in a circle ready to begin and did not need a warm-up or any encouragement to focus on what we were doing. If we had had time to continue workshops in this class, we would have continued to work on conflict resolution. The teacher felt that the communication skills of the class had improved a great deal.

3. Another Fourth Grade Class in East Harlem, New York City

One class we worked with during the 1974–75 school year was in East Harlem. At the semester break this fourth grade class lost half its students and gained a larger half of another class, forcing us to begin again. We wanted to give the new students what we had already done, but also move into new areas with the old students. We felt the biggest problem in both groups was the lack of self-esteem and mutual respect, so we decided to spend most of the semester on affirmation.

We began with singing and name games to introduce ourselves, get to know the new children and develop a sense of community. The old members of the class were eager to teach the newcomers songs and loosening-up activities. This affirmed the old members who felt secure enough to teach the songs and games and gave the new students more attention than was possible in the first semester.

We did silhouette drawings, put them on the wall to admire and came up with five positive statements about each child, which we pasted on the silhouettes. We spent a lot of time on affirmation in large and small groups. We started with simple questions, such as "What's one thing you had fun doing last weekend?" Next children pantomimed things they like to do while others guessed what they were. We tried small group interviews in which children chose topics for interviews, while others contributed questions to ask. Children took turns so everyone had a chance to be interviewed and to ask questions.

We worked on cooperation by building monsters and machines in small groups and then sharing them with the class. We emphasized affirmation, and the children did not hesitate to praise each other's work. We took slides of the creations, resulting in further acclaim by the class.

By the end of the eighth week there was a sense of community, playfulness and mutual affirmation. We sensed a need for an in-depth project, so we began *Affirmation Notebooks,* which we continued for the remaining seven weeks of the program. We had children create one or two notebook pages at each session, using the same sequence as they are presented in chapter eleven. Notebook pages were done in small groups, discussing each one in turn. Children eagerly sought and offered help with spelling, and took great pride in the appearance of their sheets. They also valued each other and shared materials consistently. Along with the *Affirmation Notebook,* we did loosening-up and cooperation games such as *Zoom, Musical Laps, Pantomimes* and *Telephone*.

We sang at every session, handing out lyric sheets to help the children learn new songs. The children liked the sheets so much that they put them in their *Affirmation Notebooks.* We also had the children perform puppet shows before the puppets were put in the notebooks.

At the last session we sang all the songs we knew, had written evaluations in small groups and put together the *Affirmation Notebooks.* The activities children liked most were *Silhouettes, Affirmation Notebook* covers, *Balloon Sheets, T-shirts,* having pictures taken, making puppets, *Machine Building* and *Telephone*.

4. A Second Grade Class in East Harlem, New York City

We had worked with the teacher of this class before, but this year our goal was to integrate our techniques into classroom life and the curriculum. After starting out with a few sessions of loosening-up exercises, we moved to community building, followed by three sessions on conflict story reading and discussions of solutions.

We decided to work together with other classes to present a Christmas show for the lower grades. The production included skits, puppet shows, a slide show and singing. After the holidays, we devoted several sessions to the *Affirmation Notebook.* We started out with drawing exercises and gradually moved to writing. We saw this as a way to improve reading and writing skills. The writing exercises included *Fruit I Like, Animals I Like, Weather I Like, My Family Tree* and *Questions About Me.* We also continued to sing together.

In February we used *Affirmation Valentines* as a reading and writing project. The teacher was concerned about upcoming reading tests and wanted to prepare her class in a way that was both affirming and fun. We worked together to create a structure to do this. The teacher used old reading tests to find model questions. We had children make up their own tests to help them understand the structure and give them practice taking tests. The first week we used the *Word Game* and the second week the *Fill-In-the-Blank Word Game* and the *Sentence Game.* (All of these are described on page 48.) In each game children chose a picture, pasted it on a sheet of paper and made up words or sentences, one of which described the picture. Children shared their games with the class, which tried to guess the correct word or sentence and then applauded. The *Picture Vocabulary Games* were both affirming to individuals and effective practice for reading tests.

Toward the end of the year we went on field trips and had children write positive things about them. We also did arts and crafts including weavings and collages for Mother's Day. As a writing project we made Mother's Day cards.

The last few weeks we spent on cooperation exercises such as *Community Music Making* for which each child made an instrument. The students planned the last session to include the games and songs they enjoyed most.

5. An In-Service Teacher Course in Montclair, New Jersey

We gave a series of eighteen workshops to teachers and principals in the Montclair school system, divided into two in-service courses. The first was on self-concept development and the second on conflict resolution. The format of the conflict resolution course involved discussions dealing with conflicts that teachers had to cope with. The following is a review of the conflict resolution course.

The goal of the first session was to introduce the participants, get them to feel comfortable with each other and begin to discuss the elements of conflict. We used *Conflict Story Reading* and had a brainstorming on the causes of conflict.

The second session began with a review and categorization of the brainstorming ideas. We discussed the use of puppetry and comic strips with children.

The third session focused on roleplaying. We introduced the techniques of *Role Reversal* and *Quick Decision Roleplaying*. We discussed how to set up a roleplay and the alternatives of having the teacher choose the scenario or allowing the class to brainstorm situations. We covered other aspects of roleplaying, such as the importance of stating the issue clearly and how to select the characters and set the scene. We pointed out how roleplaying helps children find alternative solutions to conflicts, analyze communication and discern the motives and feelings of others.

In the fourth session, we did skits and examined the many uses of light-and-livelies. We discussed the differences between skits and roleplays and did an extended roleplay. We discussed how to plan a session to meet the needs of the class.

In the fifth session we did *Goal Wish Problem Solving* and introduced *Conflict Story Writing*. In the sixth session we discussed establishing a pattern for dealing with conflict in the classroom. We mentioned the use of workshops and class meetings. By this time teachers were already using some of these techniques in their classrooms so the discussions included their personal experiences.

The next two sessions were spent roleplaying specific types of conflicts including child-child, adult-adult, teacher-child and parent-child. We talked about using various conflict resolution techniques with children in addition to considering the conflicts themselves.

The final session included a review of the previous eight weeks, an intensive evaluation and a concluding discussion of conflict resolution. Teachers were especially proud of having come up with so many alternatives for dealing with conflict in the classroom.

6. Some New Directions

New directions taken by the CCRC program include mediation training and bias awareness. One example of CCRC's mediation work is a lunchtime training for a group of six children from a fifth grade class. The children received eight weeks of training ($1\frac{1}{2}$ hours per week) and then mediated conflicts in their classroom and on the school playground. The following year the program expanded as two schools adopted school-wide mediation programs. Students with previous CCRC experience were chosen to be mediators, trained in ten 2-hour sessions, and given lunchtime duty in both schools.

In the field of bias awareness, CCRC introduced activities centering on putdowns, name calling and prejudice. We also had speakers and workshop facilitators make presentations from a Native American perspective. A teacher we had previously worked with invited us to do a multicultural presentation for her class. We presented a slideshow on Yugoslavia, and two Yugoslav children in the class were affirmed by the beautiful pictures. We talked about the language, food and clothing of Yugoslavia. The response was so positive that we found slideshows on the Netherlands, France, Germany, Switzerland and the Soviet Union and presented them to other classes. We hope to continue this process.

Children's Growth toward Cooperation: The Teacher's Role

Loren D. Weybright
City College of New York

This paper examines the relationship between the developmental point of view and a supportive atmosphere which encourages the growth of affirmation, communication, cooperation and conflict resolution. There are several developmental themes central to Jean Piaget's ideas about the growth of cooperation and thinking which have direct implications for those who work with children (and adults). The first theme is that children's thinking and their point of view of the world are quite different from adults' thinking. These differences are expressed in terms of successive stages of development.

The second theme is that the development of thinking and a cooperative point of view is based upon the process of action and interaction. A third theme describes the importance of observing children's actions, language and development in general. Contrary to what was once assumed, Piaget discovered not only that children know less than adults but that there are fundamental differences in the form and pattern of thought, roughly defined according to age. The very framework or what Piaget calls the "structure" of children's ideas about their physical and social world differs in essential, often dramatic ways from an adult's point of view. A preschooler for example called to his father, "Get behind me, daddy, so they can't see you." A three-year-old proclaimed, "I have feet, you have feet, Curtis don't have feet. He isn't here."

From a young child's point of view, what she sees, everybody sees. What she doesn't see doesn't have much meaning. Piaget describes this as egocentric thinking. During the preschool years, roughly from two through five or seven years of age, the child literally "centers" or focuses on one dimension, one point of view (his own), and expects others to do the same. The preschooler (and many primary grade children) will, when retelling a story or giving directions, provide only a bare account of the entire episode. He or she assumes the listener knows all that he or she knows, so why restate the obvious! The older child begins to understand that there are clearly points of view other than one's own.

The different points of view expressed characterize the two stages in the development of social cooperation. Piaget (1932) describes these stages as the two moralities of childhood, the morality of adult constraint and the morality of cooperation.

Constraint and Egocentrism

Children's judgments in the morality of constraint appear to be held back by the external rules of adult authority. Rules, they believe, can't be changed. A child adapts to adult constraint by placing rules on the level of moral absolutes, i.e., he or she determines wrongdoing on the basis of external evidence, not internal motives. For example, the child feels that someone who broke many glasses by accident should receive more punishment than someone who broke only a few glasses, regardless of motive. The child focuses on the letter of the law rather than considering the spirit behind it. In terms of the child's ideas about justice, authority itself is in command and the child is not able to see the possibility of an equitable distribution of sanctions or rewards (Piaget, 1932).

Age and Stage

The first stage of adult constraint lasts from birth to around seven or eight years of age, followed by the stage of cooperation. The age at which the morality of cooperation first appears varies widely among children and varies within any one child's judgments about different conflict situations. I have observed six-year-olds in cooperative play who showed true collaborative efforts in constructing a playhouse. The primary importance of the concept of stages is that the sequence remains invariant.

Cooperation

The morality of cooperation is seen among children who consider rules that are based on rational social conventions, rules which serve group rather than individual goals. These older children, from about age seven onward, will seek group consensus of a rule in their games. In *Monster Making* they would seek a common goal toward a cooperatively developed drawing of a monster rather than each child drawing his own arms and legs unrelated to the whole.

In terms of wrongdoing, it is judged on the basis of motive and external evidence. Children playing chess for example were observed to carefully follow the rules, with the exception that some were "speaking on the game." They gave helpful hints to a new player, showing her which moves to make, even though it was against the rules to do so. The special circumstance, in this case teaching a new player, overruled the requirement that the spectators were not to comment on the players' moves.

In terms of justice, the children are able to place their judgment of behavior in a social context, seen in terms of equality for all (Piaget, 1932). In discussing a conflict situation, mid-primary age children on this level of development would propose solutions where all participants must be treated equally no matter what the circumstances. It is only later that children are able to temper equality with equity which accounts for extenuating circumstances.

The development of cooperation has its roots in the preschool years as the children share toys, friends, feelings and ideas. But sharing at this age is limited to instances where the children have a common goal. At the primary grade level children develop shared goals and feelings of respect and sympathy. It is here they are first able to imagine a point of view other than their own. They are able to think of an action or idea outside of themselves. By the intermediate grade level we can see the development of true cooperation based on group consensus. These older children for example purposefully seek peer recognition for their ideas. "We could build the monster with a golden head, couldn't we?" "Yeah, and then we could have a golden shield to match."

Awareness and Action

A difference between knowing the "right" solution and acting on that solution is clearly seen in the development of both cooperation and thinking. The development of true cooperation depends upon intention and deliberation grounded in direct experience close to children's own areas of interest. Brearly (1970) suggests that it is relatively easy for young children to be *taught* to say "I'm sorry" when their play gets rough and someone gets hurt. It is entirely another matter, however, to understand the feelings of sorrow and to grasp and empathize with the feelings of the other child in that moment of hurt.

In summary, the growth toward cooperation is primarily concerned with understanding another person's point of view. The child's ability to place himself in "another person's shoes" only gradually appears through social interaction with peers and adults in a variety of settings. This ability is dependent partially upon the quality of experience a child has had, the quality of the interaction.

Action and Interaction

Successive stages need not be the focus of the teacher's observations of children's social development. The direction and process of action and interaction according to Brearly (1970) count for more than anything else. The stages are age-specific. The central theme of action and interaction is a process that recurs throughout all ages. Piaget's conception of the growth of intelligence and the development of cooperation as active processes is a central notion in his theory. The activity of the child (or adult) is expressed through two types of actions: first, as external sensory and motor investigations of the child's surroundings, such as exploring the texture of clay or the feel of water; and second, as internal thinking actions such as comparing (sand and water), counting, or matching (my idea with yours).

An important example of action and interaction is seen in roleplaying, where the child who plays the role helps to internalize the meaning of another child's action. If the child experiences an event in a roleplay setting (for example the role of a child who has been excluded), it provides him or her with a common base of experience with another child (the one who really was excluded).

Experience in roleplay, for example, is not understood in the same way at different ages. The young child, not able to get outside of herself, can only appreciate the experience if it has matched her own. The older child, now able to construct a point of view other than his own, may truly empathize with the modeled role. The younger child only focuses on one aspect of the role at a time, reflecting his or her one-dimensional point of view. The older child (seven through ten years of age) is able to account for several dimensions of the experience at once in his or her explanation of equality. The older child knows that the rules must meet the test of group consensus.

The importance of action and interaction is summarized by Piaget when he proposes that in order for children to develop intelligence (or cooperation), they must construct it themselves. This active knowing behavior can be seen in the preschooler as he or she begins to establish the important concept of a mother's or father's role. At first it is a limited view of a one-dimensional role: a mother can only be a housekeeper. It is only later understood that a mother can be both a doctor and a housekeeper.

The third theme is about the importance of observing for both the teacher and child. Piaget's (1972) clinical method of observing children's development provides the teacher-observer with an appropriate starting point for conducting an objective analysis of children's social interaction. The CCRC program activities provide an opportunity for extending the process to children's own active observation.

The central aim of Piaget's method is to uncover the trend, the basic structure of children's actions and social interactions. The observer may begin by focusing on one child or activity and regularly recording the language and actions that occur for a brief period each day or for several days. The observer, by examining one child's actions and words as a whole piece, is able to establish an inventory of that child's ideas and explanations. The inventory could take the form of a log or an anecdotal record, kept close at hand for easy note taking. The inventory gathered over long-term observations of the child in many situations may then be used to determine patterns in that child's growth. It is the long-range view of a child's growth that will allow the teacher to place the developmental achievements of an individual in proper perspective.

Children's observations, an integral part of the CCRC program, are described in chapter nine, "Do You Hear Me?" Children's (and adults') objective observation of social and physical interactions is the implied goal of such activities as *Know Your Orange*, while the *Eyewitness Skit* depends upon an already-rehearsed activity that suddenly "happens" in front of a group. Afterward the group tries to describe the details of what happened. It usually results in the children relating many different stories of what occurred.

A child's description of an orange or an event is based upon his or her point of view. An egocentric child's descriptive observations are characterized by fragmentary statements which emphasize only one aspect of an object or an event. The child at the cooperative (or what Piaget calls the concrete) level can provide a multidimensional description of the orange. She begins to accept as valid another person's point of view of a recent event.

Brearly (1970) shows how observations are determined partly by past experience which is personal and internalized, and partly by the test of reliability, a social act in which one's own observation is confirmed or disputed by another person's observation. To encourage observational learning, Brearly recommends that children too keep records or logs. Records may be kept on many processes and objects, including changes in plants or pets and growth in animals or children. These observations serve to develop awareness of the children's own experience and to encourage growth toward the acceptance of another person's observation as a valid point of view.

The teacher's role in supporting children's observations of physical or social events is to document and describe children's interests and ideas, to extend their thoughts and actions, to pose questions based on children's own questions, and to integrate experience and ideas. The gradual appearance of cooperation for example depends on the child's and teacher's ability to understand another person's idea and to listen.

The development of communication skills is critical in the resolution of conflict. Conflicts often originate in the failure of communication or in the lack of exchange of ideas. The teacher can support the development of communication by providing an opportunity for true dialogue to occur. This is strengthened through careful recording and documentation of children's language samples in ordinary experience. The samples need not be extensive. Five or ten minutes a day of observation, focused on one or two children or events, often show the observer a pattern in communication never noticed before. The teacher may observe for example that the role of a listener is tied to the egocentric thinking of a young child. When that child retells a story, he accounts only for single isolated elements, not an integrated whole. The essence of listening is the exchange of meaning among equals. If the teacher provides an atmosphere that improves the flow of meaning among children and adults, she or he will be able to reduce the potential for conflict. Teachers who do observe children regularly have become convinced of the importance of action and social interaction in independent (play) and organized (games) activities for the intellectual and social development of the child.

Summary

The development of children's ideas and practice of cooperation is closely related to the growth of affirmation, communication, problem solving and thinking in general. This relationship may be described in terms of several developmental themes. The first theme demonstrates that children's thinking is different from adults' thinking in terms of its structure or framework. Piaget proposed that these structures (e.g., egocentrism, cooperation, justice) develop through a sequence of stages, a sequence found to be invariant across cultures. While the first theme describes the *differences* in patterns of the way children and adults think, the second theme shows similarities in the processes supporting the development of thought.

Piaget's notion of the growth of cooperation and intelligence is an active process, which develops through the action and interaction of childhood. The child and adult must construct their own patterns of thought or intelligence, not through passive and didactic instruction, but through personal action on his or her surroundings and through social interaction and cooperation with others.

Piaget (1932) speaks directly to those who work with children as he describes the importance of individual action and social cooperation: "Let us therefore try to create in the school a place where individual experimentation and reflection carried out in common come to each other's aid and balance one another" (page 404).

The third theme of observing children draws upon the clinical interview and the questions concerning the development of children's ideas about rules in their play. Observing and questioning children in an unstructured, developmental context allows (classroom) practice to illuminate theory.

Note: The preceding paper was written in 1977. The field of moral development has been subsequently expanded and developed by others, see in particular Carol Gilligan, *In a Different Voice* (Cambridge: Harvard University Press, 1982).

References

Brearly, M., ed. 1970. *The Teaching of Young Children: Some Applications of Piaget's Learning Theory*. New York: Schocken Books.

Piaget, J. 1972. *The Child's Conception of the World*. Totowa, NJ: Littlefield, Adams. Original French edition, 1924.

Piaget, J. 1932. *The Moral Judgment of the Child*. New York: Harcourt Brace Jovanovich.

Weybright, L. 1976. "The Development of Play and Logical Thinking: The Teacher as Researcher." *The Urban Review* 9(2): 133–140.

Weybright, L. 1976. *Piaget and Children's Play*. Fairlawn, NJ: JAB Press.

Children's Creative Response to Conflict: A Developmental Point of View

A graduate course held at City College of New York, School of Education

Several people requested information on the content of the course given at CCNY. While there is a more extensive report in the newsletter *Sharing Space* (vol. 1, no. 2), the following summary gives a background and rationale for the course.

Background

Loren Weybright, a professor at City College, frequently visited P.S. 75 in connection with the Open Corridor program. He learned about the Children's Creative Response to Conflict program through talking with teachers and visiting classes in which CCRC staff were conducting workshops. Loren is a Piaget specialist and very interested in game theory as it relates to the moral development of children. As a researcher, he developed the idea of combining the CCRC philosophy and techniques with moral development philosophy. He set about getting approval for the course. The pilot course took place in the fall of 1976 with fifteen students, most of whom were teachers. The course was designed to help teachers understand theory and plan techniques within a developmental framework to establish a cooperative, trusting classroom environment in which children can explore creative solutions to conflict.

Rationale

The course is based upon the following assumptions:
1. Teachers work within a developmental framework to support and examine the origins of children's ideas and practice in the four areas of cooperation, affirmation, communication and conflict resolution.
2. When people are given responsibility to make their own decisions in a classroom, they have a personal commitment to the development of the class structure. Once people take responsibility for their own decisions, through cooperation and social interaction they begin to understand the strength of the individual and the power of the group.
3. Through an awareness of individual and group capabilities, adults are better able to support children's investigations to extend their needs and capabilities.
4. Cognitive and moral development, exhibited in cooperation and response to conflict, occurs through action and social interaction. In order for cognitive and moral structures to develop, children and adults must construct them. This course is designed for students to reconstruct this development through observing, listening to, participating in and evaluating children's activities. They develop the rationale and means to apply the techniques to support children's (and their own) growth. They develop alternative ways of integrating cooperation and conflict resolution into the total structure of the life of the classroom.

Course Outline

Session 1
Agenda
Introduction: One thing you like to do
Project introduction and theory

Structure details and handouts
Three Question Interview
Evaluation

Session 2
Agenda and Logistics
Pop-up Name Game
Pantomime One Thing You Like to Do
Telephone
Small Group Cooperation Drawing
Evaluation
Session 3
Agenda
Logistics
New-and-Goods
Expectation sharing
Introduction to conflict resolution
Discussion
Evaluation
Session 4
Agenda and Logistics
New-and-Goods
Machine Building
Discussion of developmental theory
Evaluation
Session 5
New-and-Goods: One book you enjoyed
  reading
Agenda and Logistics
In small groups, share a time you enjoyed
  learning something
Elephant and Palm Tree
Grab Bag Dramatics
Discussion
Evaluation
Session 6
New-and-Goods
Agenda
Musical Laps
Relating affirmation to cooperation
Affirmation Notebook Cover
Dealing with putdowns
Evaluation
Session 7
Animal Name Tags
Agenda and Logistics
Discussion of *Affirmation Notebook Covers*
Touch Blue
Affirmation T-shirt
Brainstorming *Affirmation Notebook* pages
Affirmation Interviewing
Evaluation
Session 8
New-and-Goods
Agenda
Introduction to communication
Paraphrasing in small groups: What does
  communication mean to you?
Summary of paraphrasing

Discussion
Evaluation
Session 9
New-and-Goods
Agenda
Fishbowl: How do you break up fights?
Introduction to conflict resolution
Discussion
Singing
Evaluation
Session 10
New-and-Goods
Agenda
Brainstorming the causes of conflict
Quick Decision Roleplays
Discussion
Evaluation
Session 11
What's something good that has happened in
  your class?
My Bonnie
Conflict Story Reading: Goggles by Ezra Jack
  Keats
Brainstorming for a Saturday get-together
Discussion
Evaluation
Session 12
What's one color you like, and what does it
  mean to you?
Discussion of moral development
Human Pretzel
Conflict Resolution Skit
Discussion
Evaluation
Session 13
What's one thing you like about this group?
Discussion of the teacher's role in moral
  development
Roleplaying
Discussion
Evaluation
Session 14
Agenda
New-and-Goods
Goal Wish Problem Solving
Elephant and Palm Tree
Brainstorming activities you'd like to do
Discussion
Evaluation
Session 15
Affirmation Sharing: Say three things you like
  about yourself to your partner
Sin of Commission Game
Evaluation
Closing Circle

After the Course

The class got together one Saturday after the course was completed. We did several longer activities that we had not had time to do before. The class members decided to form an ongoing study group to meet monthly. We alternated meeting at each other's houses, and students took full responsibility for planning and facilitating the meetings. Thus the study group became a place for teachers to practice facilitation in a safe atmosphere. Students requested that the study group include half experiential activities and half discussion. Some sessions were devoted to book discussions. The study group was an important model of teacher support.

Building Friendship in the Classroom

Singing, Classroom Atmosphere and Conflict Resolution

As a workshop facilitator with the Children's Creative Response to Conflict (CCRC) program, I have wanted for a long time to join with others in putting together a book of songs for teachers or group leaders to use with children. I feel fortunate to have worked with Evelyn Weiss and Nancy Silber in helping to create *Children's Songs for a Friendly Planet,* a book whose purposes parallel our own. The social sciences and peace groups have long held that peace begins with caring about others as well as ourselves, and that it can be maintained whether among individuals or nations through the use of a variety of creative approaches to conflict resolution.

We have found singing to be a great asset in our work with children. In itself, singing is an excellent group-building activity in which each one can participate without the need to be musically talented. In singing together each person shares in creating a satisfying whole in which all can take pride. Singing also helps energize positive feelings. In our experience, positive feelings tend to escalate, much as negative ones tend to do. The logical alternative then is to put our energy into building positive feelings. It is no more difficult, and it is more conducive to learning than coping with negative feelings and angry encounters.

While the primary goal of the program is to help teachers help children to find creative solutions to conflict, CCRC has received much support not only from the teaching profession but from the peace education and nonviolence movements. The program originated in the Quaker Project on Community Conflict (QPCC) which was funded by the New York Society of Friends. QPCC had spent several years giving nonviolence training, in which peacekeeping skills were learned by those who would help keep violence from breaking out in the many mass demonstrations of the sixties and early seventies. Several people in this core soon realized that nonviolence theory could be applied to young children.

When CCRC initiated its program in 1972, it focused on conflict resolution activities—skits, roleplaying and brainstorming solutions to conflict. But it soon became clear that it is vitally important to first build a sense of community to enable children to feel comfortable in their group and safe enough to share their feelings about conflict. So for both classrooms and teacher workshops a series of cooperative activities was devised to help develop a positive sense of group as the initial part of the program. These activities included and still include cooperative drawings of all sorts, improvisational theater activities and others, from making fruit salad to making scarecrows. In these activities everyone contributes to a final product. This increases positive feelings about oneself and others.

The CCRC program developed a second theme, communication, in response to the concern of so many teachers over the lack of listening skills among children in their classes. CCRC then focused on listening, speaking and observation skills, all of which can be learned and improved with practice. Communication skills are also an indispensable ingredient of conflict resolution. Children enjoy challenging communication activities such as *Paraphrasing* (saying it another way) or *Three Things that Have Changed,* an observation game in which children carefully observe each other, change three things about themselves and then try to guess what each other has changed. *Direction Following* is another listening game wherein children practice following fun directions.

Affirmation activities are frequently very direct. Children say what they like to do, what they are proud of or are adept at. The more children practice, the easier it becomes for them to affirm themselves and each other. Keeping *Affirmation Notebooks,* full of pages about positive qualities written by the individual or others in the class, can go on throughout the year. Creating silhouette drawings, *Affirmation Commercials* and *Affirmation Pantomimes* are activities that encourage children to feel positive about themselves and others. In *Affirmation Interviews,* where one child talks about him/herself with the whole group's full attention, there is group building going on because the whole group is doing something positive for one individual. Listening skills are improving because all feel the need to concentrate, and the child being interviewed is being affirmed. We can see listening and conversing

(Reprinted in part from *Children's Songs for a Friendly Planet,* 1986. Used by permission.)

skills improve, which alone is important, but when children begin to attain a better self-concept the change is remarkable. Feeling better about themselves, children grow in other areas of their lives—socially, academically and emotionally. The better they feel about themselves, the better they feel about others and the more able they are to express their feelings and viewpoints when the need for conflict resolution arises.

While the four CCRC themes are interrelated, they are also developmental. CCRC workshops begin with *group-building activities,* then move to simple, objective *communication skill-building activities,* then to *affirmation of self and others.* The self-concept (affirmation) activities become progressively more risk taking. In time a cooperative mood develops as children begin to feel better about themselves individually and as group members. Within the context of these positive group feelings, creative conflict resolution activities are most successful. The same sequence and intertwining of the themes apply in our teacher workshops as well, which are a major part of the CCRC program. In children's groups we use skits, puppetry, roleplaying, videotaping of conflict scenarios, stories and comic strips to examine various alternatives to many types of conflict. After children have had a variety of these practice experiences, they are better prepared to deal with real-life conflicts. Later these creative responses to conflict can be applied to school or community situations. As we discuss conflicts, children often make the connection between problems on a personal, group, community, national or international level. Older children particularly show concerns over world problems such as hunger and the possibility of nuclear war.

With the above overview in mind, it is readily seen how CCRC has found singing to be an invaluable group builder. Some songs are obviously and directly about a cooperative spirit. One such song is the camp favorite *The More We Get Together:*

The More We Get Together

The more we get together, together, together
The more we get together the happier we'll be.
For your friends are my friends, and my friends are your friends,
The more we get together the happier we'll be.

Children can repeat the song several times, using alternate key words (*play, sing, work,* etc.) in place of *get.* This can be used as a name-learning song too, as children go around the class or group, beginning at the third line and singing the names of children in the room: "There's Arthur and Monica and Judy and Ali, and Joyce and Phoebe and Bobby and Steven. There's Marion. . . ." Finally the last line is sung.

Singing can also be effective when it encourages people to laugh or share a sense of fun. Laughter reduces tension, helps people to feel better about themselves and in that sense it can serve as a preventive method in conflict resolution. When people laugh together at the same things they feel a sense of cohesion. All are reacting enjoyably together, all are in on the same joke and not at the expense of anyone. One silly song, which is next to impossible for most groups to sing at first without laughter, is *Black Socks.* Children can share in the fun of discovering the joke if the teacher presents it as serious the first time the song is sung to the class.

Black Socks

Enjoyment can continue in another way, as one part of the group repetitiously sings the final words "Not yet, not yet, not yet . . ." and the rest of the group sings the song itself over and over. It is group building to have the song end by gradually fading out with numerous "not yets."

Another fun nonsense song is the old English tune, *One Bottle of Pop:*

One Bottle of Pop

Traditional

This song can be sung over and over again. A variation is to "sing" the song silently except for the last word of each verse: *pop, full,* and *pot.* People must really exercise restraint to carry through this prescript.

Another fun song for young children is *Have a Plate of Soup*.

Have a Plate of Soup

Words and music copyright 1985 by Evelyn Weiss. Used by permission.

Have a plate of soup and sand - wich - es,

Have a plate of soup to - day. Take it on the trol - ley,

Take it on the train. If you like it hot don't

take it in the rain. Won't you have a plate of soup,

soup - y, soup - y soup? Have a plate of soup to - day

Children can create pantomimes to this song, "spooning" soup, "bouncing" with it on the trolley, train or bus, or "balancing" it while walking. They can make up alternate lyrics in place of *sandwiches: noodles, glub glub, dumplings*, etc.

Songs which include motions afford a welcome change of pace. When people enjoy the same action together they tend to feel positive about being together. Motion songs can also be used as light-and-lively activities, those which help energize people who have been seated for too long a time. Light-and-livelies help prevent restlessness which can lead to unnecessary conflict or lack of interest in the central involvement of the group. One such favorite motion song is *My Bonnie Lies over the Ocean*.

My Bonnie Lies over the Ocean

Traditional

My   Bon - nie lies   o - ver   the   o - cean, ———   My
Bon-nie   lies   o - ver   the   sea. ———   My   Bon-nie lies
o - ver   the   o - cean, ———   Oh, bring back my   Bon-nie   to
me. ———   Bring   back,   bring   back,   Bring back my
Bon-nie to   me, to   me.   back, Oh, bring back my Bon-nie   to   me.

Once the song is learned, the lively activity can be introduced. Instead of just singing, the group stands up (or if standing, sits down) on the sound of each word that begins with the letter *b*. Stepping up the pace of the song on successive verses makes for more enjoyment.

Head, Shoulders, Knees and Toes

Tune: Tavern in the Town

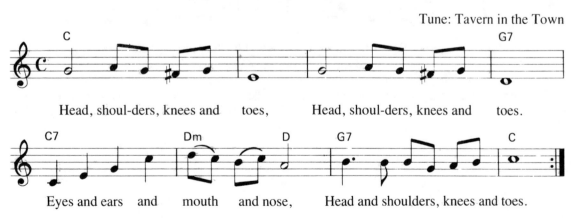

Head, shoul-ders, knees and   toes,   Head, shoul-ders, knees and   toes.
Eyes and ears   and   mouth   and nose,   Head and shoulders, knees and toes.

103

The motions consist of pointing or reaching to the parts of the body mentioned. It makes for amusement when the tempo of the song is increased as it is repeated several times. It is fun when, one by one, the last body part is dropped from each line as the song is repeated. By the fifth verse, all are moving to the song but not singing it aloud.

One last category is those songs that directly affirm individuals, that help people to feel better about themselves and others. One very positive upbeat song is *You Can Make the Sun Shine,* which can be sung rain or shine.

You Can Make the Sun Shine

Children can recall happy times spent indoors or elsewhere on bad-weather days, share these recollections, or choose to recall such times through picture-drawings, perhaps for a group-to-talk-about display.

I Like You is another such song; it is sung to the verse of *Skip to My Lou*.

I Like You

1. I like you; there's no doubt about it.
   I like you; there's no doubt about it.
   I like you; there's no doubt about it.
   You are my good friend.

2. You like me; there's no doubt about it.
   You like me; there's no doubt about it.
   You like me; there's no doubt about it.
   I am your good friend.

3. I like me; there's no doubt about it.
   I like me; there's no doubt about it.
   I like me; there's no doubt about it.
   I am my good friend.

It is important that children choose their partners for the song so that they feel comfortable saying "I like you." In the first verse as "I like you" is sung, children point to their partners; in all verses on "no doubt about it," they move open hands in the air while shaking heads indicating no; on "I am your good friend" partners shake hands. In the second verse as "you like me" is sung, children point first to their partners and then to themselves. In the last verse children point to themselves, and on "I am my good friend" hug themselves. This song should be used only after children have shared a great deal of self-and others-affirmation, in which case it can be a moving experience. Otherwise it could prove ineffective. Another song, *Child of the Universe,* is an affirmation of all people in the world and of the right of all to share in the bounty of our part of the universe: the earth including the atmosphere, the sun, and the moon, the latter a source of light for farmers and those in rural and polar regions. The song can be sung as a round.

Child of the Universe

Excerpt from *Desiderata* by Max Ehrmann

Lyrics adapted by Helen Hafner   Tune: White Coral Bells (two-part round)

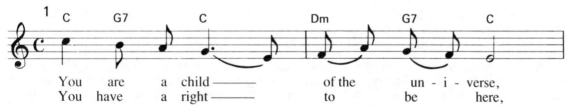

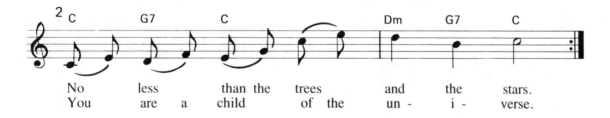

Copyright by Helen Hafner. Used by permission.

Children can name the natural parts of the earth, those that cover great areas of the earth's surface and also those elements or phenomena—sunlight, atmosphere, clouds, rain, growth, etc.—that produce and sustain all life. Children might make a mural or wall diagram showing many of these natural and functional elements upon which we are all dependent. That each of us has a right to a fair share of the earth's resources is universally acknowledged in a declaration made by an official and large majority of the representatives of the nations of the world. (The representatives of more than half of the world's nations so voted in the establishment of the Universal Declaration of Human Rights by the United Nations General Assembly in 1948. Eleanor Roosevelt was the lead proponent of this enduring document and she is credited with its successful passage during the time she served as the United States representative to the United Nations.)

The Toast has a universal quality, affirming the need of people everywhere for the warmth and caring of friends, family and wider group associations.

The Toast

Words traditional

Music by Priscilla Prutzman

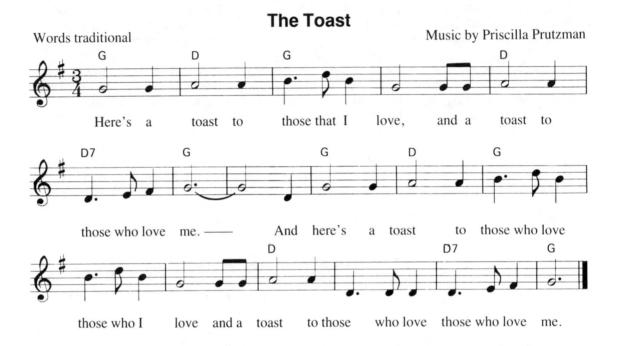

This is a good song for singing at group parties, before long weekends or vacations, or when the mood strikes. There are many positive ways of using music with children and many kinds of activities other than music that can be used to develop CCRC themes. Those set out here are just a few ideas.

Here's a toast to all your good ideas.

Priscilla Prutzman
Children's Creative Response to Conflict

Songs We Use

Too-da-la

Good	morning to you,	Too-da-la,	too-da-la,	too-da-la,
Good	morning to Mary,	Too-da-la,	too-da-la,	too-da-la,
We	are nice and early,	Too-da-la,	too-da-la,	too-da-la,

Good	morning to you,	Too-da-la,	too-da-la-la,	la-dy.
Good	morning to Bobby,	Too-da-la,	too-da-la my	dai-sy.
You	are early too,	Too-da-la,	too-da-la my	dai-sy.

This song can be sung over and over without stopping, adding something about each child in the room. The children may take turns adding something about themselves: "I have a new green dress, I'm wearing it today," or "I like cherry pie," or "I found a penny." Self-affirmation may be encouraged: "Daddy says I sing well," or verses may be added by others in the group affirming positive traits or values, so that children have an added sense of mutual support and appreciation: "Susan has a nice smile."

Too-da-la can also be used at play to sing about what each child is doing: "I'm turning round, around and around." Or the reverse can be tried, with each child deciding on something to sing that he or she would like to act out. The versatility of *Too-da-la* encourages the imaginations of children and teachers.

Good Morning to You

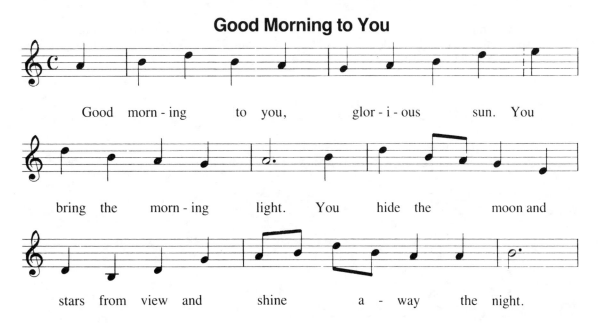

Good morn - ing to you, glor - i - ous sun. You

bring the morn - ing light. You hide the moon and

stars from view and shine a - way the night.

The preceding song is from a Waldorf nursery school. These schools are based on the philosophy of Rudolf Steiner, which looks toward the education of the whole child. Many such songs including this one use a pentatonic scale. The message of the following song, *There Is Always Something You Can Do,* can be a useful tool to get children to hear each other out when anger and hurt feelings prevail; then try for an agreement that seems fair to both sides. Children might also play-act such a scene.

There Is Always Something You Can Do

Brightly

Words and music by Sarah Pirtle

1. There is al - ways some - thing you can do, do, do   When you're
al - ways some - thing you can do, do, do   Yes it's
al - ways some - thing you can do, do, do   When you're

get - ting in a stew, stew, stew;   You can go out   for a walk
dif - fi - cult but true, true, true.   See it from each oth - er's eyes,
get - ting in a stew, stew, stew.   When you want to take a poke,

You can try to sit and talk.   There's al - ways
Find a way to com - pro - mise.   There's al - ways
Turn a - round and make a joke.   There's al - ways

some - thing you can do.   Whe - ther in a school or fam - 'ly
some - thing you can do.   You can use your smarts and not your
some - thing you can do.

ar - gu - ment,   When you feel you'd real - ly like to throw a
fist, fist, fist;   You can give that prob - lem a new twist, twist,

fit.   Don't be trapp'd by fights and fists and an - gry threats,
twist.   You can see it 'round a - bout and up - side down,

Reach out for this or - di - na - ry plan.   2. There is
Give your - self the time to find a way.   3. There is

The Woman Who Gobbled Swiss Cheese

Copyright 1984 Sarah Pirtle

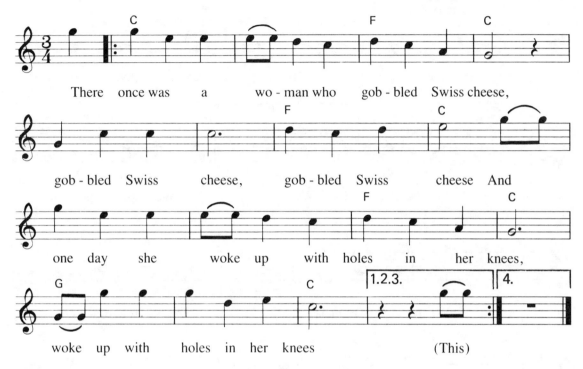

There once was a wo - man who gob - bled Swiss cheese,

gob - bled Swiss cheese, gob - bled Swiss cheese And

one day she woke up with holes in her knees,

woke up with holes in her knees (This)

The woman cried, "Help me. Oh, what can I do!
What can I do! What can I do!
When I look at my knees I see sky shining through
Now I see sky shining through."

So she ran to the doctor with ease.
Answered with ease, answered with ease.
"Swallow some tiddlywinks. They'll fill up your knees.
Tiddlywinks will fill up your knees."

So she salted some tiddlywinks and gobbled down lots.
Gobbled down lots, gobbled down lots.
Now 'stead of holes she's got green polka dots.
Now she's got green polka dots.

Under One Sky

Words and music by Ruth Pelham

CHORUS: We're all a fam-i-ly un-der one sky, We're a fam-'ly un-der one sky. We're sky.

1. Well, we're peo-ple, We're an-i-mals, We're flow-ers, We're birds in flight, Well, we're peo-ple, We're an-i-mals, We're flow-ers, and birds in flight.

CHORUS

2. Well, we're plumbers, we're doctors,
We're farmers and teachers, too. (Repeat)
CHORUS
3. We're lions, we're elephants,
We're puppies and kangaroos. (Repeat)
CHORUS

4. We're daisies, we're tulips,
We're roses, chrysanthemums. (Repeat)
CHORUS
5. Well, we're Americans, we're Russians,
We're Italians, and Vietnamese.
We're Israelis, we're Irish,
We're Africans, and we're Chinese.
CHORUS

110

Sunshine Sassafras

Words and music copyright 1975 by Fred Gee

Chorus: Sun - shine   sass - a - fras   or   pep - per - mint tea

place   a - lone   a - long   be - side   the   big   ma - ple tree

Moon - shine   can - dle light   or   fli - cker - ing   seas

while   a - go   a - way   be - yond now   just   you   and   me

Just   you   and   me   Verse 1: We stopped to   hear   the

dark   fo - rest ring   We stopped to   hear   each pe - tal sing

We danced   to   the   mu - sic   that   night

The thoughts are   so good   we   just   might

Do   it   a - gain   Do   it   a - gain

We might   just   do   it   a - gain

Verse 2: We went to see the famed starry crown
We went to see the stars falling down
We grooved to the music that night
The thoughts are so good we just might
Do it again, do it again, we might just do it again

Verse 3: We sat and felt the world spin around
We sat and felt the new silken gown
We made the music that night
The thoughts are so good we just might
Do it again, do it again, we might just do it again

Other Songs Children Enjoy

Free to Be You and Me
Kookaburra
Have You Seen the Ghost of John?
Boom, Boom, Ain't It Great to Be Crazy?
This Old Man
Save the Country
This Land Is Your Land
I'd Like to Teach the World to Sing
I Believe in Music
If You're Happy and You Know It
Michael Finnegan
Found a Peanut
Mrs. O'Leary (Fire, Fire, Fire)
My Dog Wag
If I Had a Hammer
500 Miles
When the Saints Go Marching In
Kumbaya
Rise and Shine
He's Got the Whole World in His Hands

Action Songs

The Wheels on the Bus
Punchenello
Bingo
Hokey Pokey
Six Little Ducks

Sample Workshops

Cooperation (1)

Theme
Cooperation
Goals
To develop group cooperation in drawing and to increase children's vocabulary
Materials
Large sheets of paper, crayons and/or magic markers, masking tape
Plan
1. *Three Question Interview*
2. *What Kind of Store Is This?*
3. Explain *Cooperative Store Drawing*
   Ask children to think about the following questions:
      –What kind of store do you want to draw?
      –Can the store be drawn easily by a group?
      –What are the different parts of the store?
      –What part do you want to draw?
4. Form small groups to draw stores
5. Present and explain drawings to class
6. Singing
7. Closing Circle: Name one thing you like about the stores
Comments
This is a long session that can be used with a unit on stores and occupations. It is easy to explain the pantomime game by demonstrating it. For children who have difficulty thinking of a store, it is helpful to go quickly around the circle and name stores or write them on the board. This also gives children time to decide which store to pantomime. Then children take turns pantomiming stores while others try to guess. This helps children learn new vocabulary (grocery, stationery, etc.). The teacher may want to teach more vocabulary by asking what the person who works in the store is called (clerk, chef, jeweler, etc.).

It is helpful to list the questions (step 3) on the board. Do an example so that everyone knows what to do in small groups. Ask someone in the class to paraphrase the directions. Be sure to emphasize the importance of the process (working together and having fun) rather than the product.

Cooperation (2)

Theme
Cooperation
Goals
To give children a successful experience in cooperation and to improve listening skills
Materials
One tape recorder for each small group
Plan
1. Singing in a circle
2. *Telephone*
3. Give directions for *Storytelling*
4. Form small groups
5. Have facilitators repeat directions to their groups, start tape recorders and begin storytelling.
   Playback stories to see if children listened to each other and cooperated.

6. Have groups share briefly with the class, or if time allows, playback all or part of the recordings.
7. Evaluation
8. Closing Song
Comments
The tape recorders add a new dimension to storytelling. Playing back the stories helps children see how well they listened to each other. Be sure each group has a working tape recorder. Allow each participant to choose when to finish and someone else continue the story.

Communication

Theme
Communication
Goal
To help children become better listeners and realize the value of listening through games
Materials
Costume for the magician
Plan
1. *Listening Time*
2. *The Magician*
3. *Directions Following*
4. *Telephone Game*
5. Singing
6. Evaluation
Comments
This workshop is a good way to begin work on listening skills since it has a high energy level, is enjoyable and involves everyone. All of these things help create a healthy spirit of cooperation among members of the group. *Directions Following* should last only ten or fifteen minutes since it does not involve everyone in the group. *Telephone* can be done by first doing a skit showing children who do *not* listen and then discussing the various reasons people do not hear each other. The purpose of *Telephone* is to successfully relay the original message all the way around the circle. Children love to play the game and are pleased when they get it right. Singing may be added as a closing or beginning to the workshop.

Affirmation (1)

Theme
Affirmation
Goal
To encourage children to feel positive about themselves through *Affirmation T-shirts*
Materials
Blank T-shirt sheets, crayons
Plan
1. Singing
2. *Loosening-up Game*
3. Directions:
   a. Write your name on the paper
   b. On the T-shirt draw a picture of one thing you like to do
   c. Write a word that describes you or makes you feel good (it may or may not relate to the picture)
4. Work on T-shirts in small groups
5. Show pictures to class
6. Evaluation
7. Singing
Comments
It is helpful to hand out song sheets so children can follow along with the words of the song. For children this seems to make the song more important. In doing the demonstration T-shirt drawing,

it is a good idea to have the picture ready beforehand so children don't have to wait. Some children will finish before others, so plan an activity for them. Small group leaders can ask why children chose their symbol and word, and encourage personal sharing.

Affirmation (2)

Theme
Affirmation
Goal
To make covers for affirmation notebooks that encourage children to feel good about themselves and others
Materials
Two sheets of oak tag for each child, crayons, magic markers, hole punch, brass fasteners
Plan
1. Singing in a circle
2. *Zoom*
3. *Musical Laps*
4. Explain symbol idea and demonstrate making notebook covers
   Directions:
   a. Draw a symbol of yourself (something that represents you) or of something you like to do. If you want, you can trace your hand.
   b. Go around to others and write down one nice thing about them on their covers. Sign your name if you want, but you don't have to.
   c. Be sure to punch holes in the covers so that when notebooks are assembled, the covers are properly oriented.
5. Work on notebook covers
6. Have children read one comment about themselves
7. Evaluation
8. Singing
Comments
Encourage children to help each other with spelling and tracing and to share markers and crayons. If someone *does* write something negative about another child, state clearly that this is an *affirmation* notebook. Either erase the comment or have the child start over. Be sure to affirm anyone who is put down.

Conflict Resolution (1)

Theme
Conflict resolution
Goals
1. To present a puppet show in which a problem is raised with no solution given, and to have children discuss how they feel about the conflict and create their own puppet shows with solutions to the problem
Materials
Puppets and props for puppet shows
Plan
1. *New-and-Goods*
2. *Elephant and Palm Tree*
3. Presentation of conflict
4. Form small groups to discuss solutions
5. Have groups create puppet shows with solutions to the problem
6. Have groups present puppet shows

7. Discussion of ideas offered through shows
8. Evaluation

Comments

This session runs more smoothly if children have a chance to discuss solutions before they pick up the puppets. The initial discussion in the small groups is very important, especially with younger children, because it is here that their imaginations are nurtured. Thus they are more capable of discovering creative solutions rather than playing Punch-and-Judy or only acting out a conditioned response.

Usually there is very little structured discussion after the puppet shows, but instead a general sharing of responses to them. As each puppet show has an intrinsic value and originality, there should be little competition for the best show.

Conflict Resolution (2)

Theme
Conflict Resolution
Goal
To help children understand the feelings of being excluded and excluding others, and to give children experience in finding ways to include each individual in a group
Materials
None
Plan
1. *Zoom*
2. *Gibberish Game*
3. Skits on exclusion and conflict
4. Evaluation
Comments
A possible scenario for a skit: Two friends go to a movie together. They are approached by someone who turns out to be a longtime friend of one. The friend is in town for only an hour and wants to talk privately with the other.

Gibberish should be done in a group with a strong sense of community and where children can safely take the risk of feeling excluded. It is important to discuss how children feel being excluded and excluding others. Similarly, ask the children in the skits how they feel being excluded or excluding. This is an intensive session that can lead to deep personal sharing.

Weekend Training Workshop

Goal
To give facilitators experience in many activities from the four main themes. (This workshop is also the first weekend of the training for CCRC workshop facilitators.)

Friday

Introductory Workshop (7:00–9:30 PM)
Introduction: Goals of evening and weekend
 training
Agenda and logistics
Gathering: Your name, where you're from,
 age of children you work with
Background and history of CCRC themes
Name Toss

CCRC concepts
Machine Building
Paraphrasing
Affirmation Gift Giving
Hassle Lines
How we respond to conflict
Quick Decision Making
Closing: *Rainstorm*

116

Saturday

Breakfast (8:00 AM)

Cooperation Session (9:00–11:30 AM)
Gathering: Your name and how you got it
Agenda
Cooperation concepts
Cooper Says
Cooperation Drawing
Other cooperation activities
Problem-solving concepts
Lily Pad (a children's problem-solving
   method)
Goal Wish Problem Solving
Evaluation
Closing

Lunch (noon)

Communication session (2:30–5:00)
Gathering
Agenda
Concepts of communication
listening/nonlistening
Three Things That Have Changed
Active listening
"I" statements
Other communication activities
Skits
Win-win, win-lose, lose-lose
Evaluation

Dinner (5:30 PM)

Affirmation session (7:00–9:30 PM)
Gathering: *New-and-goods*

Agenda
Pantomime One Thing You Like to Do
Pantomime variations
*Affirmation Notebook T-shirt, Buttons,
   Coat of Arms,* etc.
Affirmation Interview
I Like You
Passive, aggressive, assertive (walking,
   talking, roleplay)
Puppets, affirmation and conflict resolution
Evaluation
Closing

Sunday

Breakfast (8:00 AM)

**Conflict resolution session
   (9:00–11:30 AM)**
Gathering: *There Is Always Something You
   Can Do*
Agenda
Conflict resolution concepts
Quick Decision Roleplay
How I respond to conflict
Conflict Story Reading
Open chair
Maligned Wolf (Little Red Riding Hood
   from the wolf's point of view)
Comic Strips
Brainstorming violence in language
Other conflict resolution activities
Affirmation Notebook Covers
Evaluation
Closing

Mediation Workshop

Goals
To show the steps of mediation, to practice mediating a conflict, and to present an overview of how mediators are chosen, how various programs operate, and how mediators are trained.

Plan
Gathering: Name and background
Agenda review
Scripted mediation
Steps of mediation
Selection of mediators: three different models
Sample programs and training models
Evaluation
Closing

APPLYING TECHNIQUES TO CURRICULUM AREAS	PAGE REFERENCE	SMALL MOTOR	LARGE MOTOR	LANGUAGE ARTS	SOCIAL STUDIES	SCIENCE	MATH	ART	MUSIC	CRAFTS	DRAMA
Introductory Name Game	17			*							
Find-a-Rhyme Name Song	17			*					*		
Introduce-Your-Neighbor Game	18			*							
Introducing Yourself through a Puppet	19	*		*							
Animal Name Tags	19	*		*	*	*		*		*	
Three Question Interview	19			*							*
Loosening-Up Game	20	*	*								*
Mirror Exercise	20	*	*								*
Rebound Exercise	20	*	*								*
Human Protractor	20		*			*	*				
Mask Passing	22		*	*							*
Herman-Hermina	22	*	*								*
Pantomime This Object	22	*	*	*	*						*
Occupation Pantomime	22	*	*	*	*						*
What Kind of Store Is This?	23	*	*	*	*						*
Challenge Pantomime	23	*	*								*
Follow the Sound	23										*
Pass the Sound	23										*
Guess the Sound	23					*					*
My Bonnie	26		*						*		*
Group Cooperation Drawing	27	*		*	*			*			
Cooperative Spelling	30		*	*							
Storytelling	32			*	*						*
Group Cooperation Sound Effects Tape	32					*					*
Group Cooperation Slide Shows	32	*				*					*
Cooperative Building with Tinker Toys	33	*				*					
Rainstorm	33		*	*	*	*					*
Community Music Making	33		*						*		
Musical Laps	35			*					*		
Singing	35			*					*		
Telegraph	36		*	*	*	*					
Fishbowl	40			*	*						*
Silhouettes	46	*	*	*				*		*	
Stocking Fillers	46			*							
Affirmation Valentines	46	*	*	*				*		*	
Affirmation Cookies and Cupcakes	47			*							
Grab Bag Affirmation Notes	47	*	*	*							
Picture Games	47	*	*	*				*			
If My Feet Could Talk	48			*							*
Affirmation Notebooks	51	*	*	*	*	*	*	*			
Instrument Making	57	*	*						*	*	
Brainstorming	63			*							
Conflict Stories	63			*				*			
Fairy Tale Writing	64			*							
Utopia Gallery	64			*							
Comic Strips	65	*	*	*				*			
Comic Books	65			*				*			
Goal Wish Problem Solving	65			*							
Card Game	67			*							

CCRC Services

Workshops and Courses

An important goal of the Children's Creative Response to Conflict program is to reach as many teachers as possible. This handbook and teacher training are the two primary ways we see to implement this goal. The following workshops and courses may be adapted in content or length to fit the particular needs of your group.

Introductory workshops or Presentations
Offers a brief overview of CCRC's theory and practice. Introduces some of our techniques and uses a slide show and/or videotape to illustrate the program at work. One to two hours. An abbreviated version (slide show plus questions) of only thirty minutes is available for occasions such as faculty meetings.

One-day Workshop
Presentation of the CCRC themes of cooperation, communication, affirmation and conflict resolution using experiential exercises that participants can then use in their work with children. The afternoon session focuses on conflict resolution and problem solving.

Weekend Workshop
A more intensive development of the CCRC themes using a broader range of exercises and experiential techniques. Usually five sessions of 2½ to 3 hours.

Two-Weekend Training Workshop for Facilitators
Trains people to facilitate CCRC workshops. The first weekend focuses on the four themes and the associated skills and activities; the second weekend focuses on practicing planning and facilitating workshops.

Advanced Training for Workshop Facilitators
Open to experienced CCRC facilitators. Subjects include one or more of the following: Advanced problem-solving and conflict-resolution techniques; Bias awareness activities (activities which allow students to explore the unique and positive qualities of our own and other cultures); Mediation skills (for the school environment and especially the playground); Planning, facilitating and decision-making problems.

Fifteen-Week College Course
Offers undergraduates or graduates more extensive experience with CCRC theory and practice. Credit may be arranged.

In-Service Courses
Usually offered in eight, two-hour, weekly installments so that teachers can experiment with CCRC ideas and methods and bring their experiences back to the course.

Custom-Designed Courses
CCRC can design special workshops to meet your group's time and theme requirements. CCRC has facilitated workshops for battered women's shelters, summer camps, religious education teachers and other groups.

Other Services

Newsletter
CCRC supplements this handbook and the workshops described above with a newsletter, *Sharing Space*, published three times a year. The newsletter serves as a support system for teachers and others who are using CCRC methods in their work with children. New ideas, activities and resource materials not found in the handbook are contributed to *Sharing Space* by readers and CCRC staff. Subscription is $5 a year.

Literature Service
Books, articles and a slide show on the CCRC program are available through CCRC's literature service. We especially recommend *Children's Songs for a Friendly Planet,* with over one hundred songs and a discussion of CCRC's use of singing in the classroom ($6.75). The CCRC literature list is frequently updated and also appears in *Sharing Space;* write for the most recent edition.

119

Bibliography

Books We Have Found Helpful

Abrams, Grace Contrino. *Creative Conflict Solving for Kids*. Second edition, 1986.
Order from Peace Education Foundation, Inc., Box 19-1153, Miami Beach, FL 33119. An excellent resource book with reproducible student worksheets that can be incorporated into social studies, science and language arts curricula. Grades 4–9.

Abrams, Grace C., and Fran C. Schmidt. *Activities for Exploring Conflict and Aggression*. Out of print.
A collection of ditto masters on conflict resolution that can be used separately or as a unit.

Abrams, Grace C., and Fran C. Schmidt. *Learning Peace*. Philadelphia: Jane Addams Peace Association, 1972.
A curriculum in which a teacher poses problems and the students are encouraged to find solutions. Topics include global conflict resolution, distribution of world resources and population, nationalism, world problems and international organizations. Useful bibliography. Grades 7–12.

Abrams, Grace C., and Fran C. Schmidt. *Supplement to Learning Peace*. Philadelphia: Jane Addams Peace Association, 1974.
Additional notes, background resources, information and activities to supplement those in *Learning Peace*.

Animal Town Games.
Order from Animal Town Game Co., PO Box 2002, Santa Barbara, CA 93120. Cooperative games that also teach about the environment.

Aquino-Makles, Alexis, David C. King, and Margaret S. Branson. *Myself and Others*. 1979.
Order from Global Perspectives in Education, 218 E. 18th Street, New York, NY 10003. Ideas, activities and suggestions for teachers concerning change, communication, conflict and interdependence. Grades 1–8.

Baier, Stephen and Susan Fiske. *Educating for Peace: A Lehigh Valley Resource Guide*. Bethlehem, PA: Lehigh-Pocono Committee of Concern, 1983.
An all-inclusive book addressing curricula, teaching guides, books, films, literature and audio-visual resource guides, local and national organizations, and distributors of materials for elementary and secondary schools.

Baker, Betty. *The Pig War*. New York: Harper & Row, 1960.
An "I Can Read" book about the rivalry between two groups over an island.

Barnes, Ellen, Bill Eyman, and Maddy Brager Engolz. *Teach and Reach*. Syracuse, NY: Syracuse Human Policy Press, 1974.
An excellent reference to books, organizations, and ideas for resources in the classroom.

Beer, Jennifer, Eileen Stief, and Charles Walker. *Mediator's Handbook*. Third edition, 1987.
Order from Friends Mediation Service, 1501 Cherry Street, Philadelphia, PA 19102. A wonderful guide to mediation.

Berman, Shelley, ed. *Perspectives: A Teaching guide to the Concepts of Peace*. Cambridge, MA: Educators for Social Responsibility, 1983.
A curriculum on peace issues. Grades K–12.

Bickmore, Kathy, and Northeast Ohio Alternatives to Violence Committee. *Alternatives to Violence*.
Order from Cleveland Friends Meeting, 10916 Magnolia Drive, Cleveland, OH 44106. This is a manual for teaching peacemaking to youth and adults. The goals are to increase awareness of nonviolent alternatives, to increase understanding of the sources of violence and to develop skills among participants. The course is divided into two 20–45 minute units. It can be adapted to a wide variety of situations in public and private schools. Grades 9–12 and college.

Borba, Michelle and Craig. *Self-Esteem: A Classroom Affair*.
Order from Winston Press, 430 Oak Grove, Minneapolis, MN 55403.

Braga, Joseph and Laurie. *Children and Adults: Activities for Growing Together*. Englewood Cliffs, NJ: Prentice-Hall, 1976.
Activities that adults can do with children from birth to age six.

Brown, George. *Human Teaching for Human Learning*. New York: Viking, 1971.
George Brown, a professor of education and creativity-workshop trainer, believes that all human learning involves the intellect and the emotions, and that education should incorporate both elements for the growth of the whole person.

Brown, George, et al., *The Live Classroom: Innovation through Confluent Education and Gestalt*. New York: Viking, 1975.

Confluent education, a philosophy and teaching/learning process, combines the emotional and intellectual aspects of learning. The book contains essays on gestalt awareness and confluent education, theory, practical applications, and examples of lessons, units and course outlines.

Canfield, Jack. *101 Ways to Enhance Self-Concept in the Classroom*. Englewood Cliffs, NJ: Prentice-Hall, 1975.
  A classic in this important area and filled with excellent ideas. Deals with major themes in the study of the self and its relationship with others.

Carpenter, Susan. *A Repertoire of Peacemaking Skills*.
  Order from the Center for International Education, Hills South, University of Massachusetts, Amherst, MA 01002. An array of useful peace-promoting skills in seven major categories which can be brought to bear on many specific situations.

Castillo, Gloria. *Left-Handed Teaching: Lessons in Affective Education*. New York: Praeger, 1974.
  Proposes methods for stimulating student involvement in the learning process, regardless of socio-economic and cultural background. Provides a model for teaching that is both affective and cognitive.

Cheifetz, Dan. *Theater in My Head*. Boston: Little, Brown, 1971.
  The author's experience with a free, racially integrated theater workshop children in New York City whose purpose was to teach young children through dramatic play. Records his observations of the group's experience and outlines a lucid, practical program for helping children stretch their perceptions of themselves and the world.

Clements, Susan, Kathy Kolbe, and Eleanor Villapando. *Do-It-Yourself Critical and Creative Thinking*. Phoenix, AZ: Think Ink Publications.
  Order from Resources for the Gifted, Inc., 3421 North 44th Street, Phoenix, AZ 85018. A useful collection of thinking-skill activities in the categories of fluency, flexibility, creativity, elaboration and many others.

Cloud, Kate, et al. *Watermelons Not War—A Support Book for Parenting in the Nuclear Age*. Philadelphia: New Society, 1983.
  Activities for parents and children dealing with nuclear issues.

Crary, Elizabeth. *I Can't Wait; My Name Is Not Dummy; I Want It; and I Want to Play*. Seattle, WA: Parenting Press, 1983.
  A very usable series for preschool to first grade. Themes include time, waiting one's turn, name-calling, and sharing. These books present many options for helping children deal with their emotions. Children love these books!

Crary, Elizabeth. *Kids Can Cooperate: A Practical Guide to Teaching Problem Solving*. Seattle, WA: Parenting Press, 1986.
  This book looks at why children quarrel and offers a step-by-step negotiation process for children.

Curwin, Richard L. and Geri. *Developing Individual Values in the Classroom*. Palo Alto, CA: California Learning Handbooks, 1974.
  A good guide to values-clarification philosophy and techniques, including integration into curriculum.

De Bono, Edward. *De Bono's Thinking Course*. New York: Facts on File, 1982.
  A great book that teaches people how to think. De Bono believes thinking can be practiced and learned. Focus on perception, pattern forming, creativity and decision making.

Dewey, John. *Experience and Education*. New York: Collier, 1973.
  A brief account (120 pages) of Dewey's explanation of the role of experience in the classroom.

Dialogue: A Teaching Guide to Nuclear Issues. Cambridge, MA: Educators for Social Responsibility, 1982.
  An excellent and comprehensive teacher resource guide to raising nuclear issues in schools, from kindergarten through high school. Includes ideas on organizing a wide variety of classroom activities and dealing with the psychological effects of the arms race on children.

Dixon, Dorothy. *Teaching Children to Care: 80 Circle Time Activities for Primary Grades*. Mystic, CT: Twenty-Third.
  A field-tested guide to "caring circles" of eight to twelve children, especially for preschool to third grade, with teachers, aides, or guidance counselors in regular 20-minute sessions. Caring circles reinforce self-esteem, empathy, caring behavior, cooperation and social awareness. Personal attention and support also enhances student achievement in other areas.

Dorn, Lois. *Peace in the Family: A Workbook of Ideas and Actions*. New York: Pantheon, 1983.
  Presents concrete, practical ways for parents to encourage healthy family and child development. Gives examples of ways to talk to children and work through problems and conflicts, and offers positive alternatives and practical programs. Includes an excellent bibliography.

Drew, Naomi. *Learning the Skills of Peacemaking*. Rolling Hills Estates, CA: Jalmar Press, 1987.
  Order from Partners in Peacemaking, 120 Finderne Avenue, Bridgewater, NJ 08807. A new resource on personal, interpersonal and global peacemaking skills. Includes many ideas on appreciating cultural differences.

Eberle, Bob, and Bob Stanish. *CPS for Kids (Teaching Creative Problem Solving)*. Buffalo, NY: D.O.K.
Lots of activities for children that teach excellent problem solving processes.

Ehrlich, Harriet W., ed. *Creative Dramatics Handbook*. Philadelphia: The School District of Philadelphia, 1974.
This handbook for elementary school children incorporates goals for play and academic learning. Includes techniques that increase awareness of the five senses and deal with emotion, characterization, dialogue and story dramatization. Contains sections on using dramatic arts in math, social studies, language arts and history, and an excellent bibliography. Distributed by the National Council of Teachers of English, 1111 Kenyon Road, Urbana, IL 61801.

Einstein, Vivian. *Conflict Resolution*. St. Paul, MN: West Publishing, 1985.
A clear presentation of dispute resolution, including negotiation, mediation and arbitration. Grades 7–12 especially. Includes clarifying definitions for all mediators.

Ezer, Mel. *Training Manual for School Mediation*.
Order from Mel Ezer, College of Education, University of Hawaii at Manoa, 1776 University Avenue, Honolulu, HI 96822. Explains the process of mediation, outlines Ezer's training program, and contains mediation skills, exercises and practice simulations.

Faber, Adele, Elaine Mazlish, with Dr. Haim Ginott. *How to Talk So Kids Will Listen (and Listen So Kids Will Talk)*.
Order from the Negotiations Institute, 236 Park Avenue, NY 10169.

Fiarotta, Phyllis. *Sticks & Stones & Ice Cream Cones. The Craft Book for Children*. New York: Workman, 1975.
A good guide to imaginative projects with the simplest materials. Focuses on the child's expression of herself and her world. Good for small group projects.

Fisher, Roger and William Ury. *Getting to Yes*. Boston: Houghton Mifflin, 1981.
Valuable activities and theory on communication, conflict resolution, affirmation and cooperation.

Fluegelman, Andrew. *The New Games Book: Play Hard, Play Fair, Nobody Hurt;* and *More New Games and Playful Ideas*. New York, Doubleday: 1981.
Each book includes the non-rules for sixty games, for two to two thousand players of all ages, ranging from very quiet to very active. Also photos, history of new games, refereeing and festival-organizing suggestions, and reflections on non-competitive cooperative games and play communities.

Freire, Paulo. *Pedagogy of the Oppressed*. New York: Seabury Press, 1968.
A Brazilian educator's philosophy of getting people involved in their own decision making. Freire claims that educators have many different tasks, tools and areas to organize for a broader view. This book has been a prime source for CCRC.

Furth, Hans, and Harry Wachs. *Thinking Goes to School: Piaget's Theory in Practice*. New York: Oxford Press, 1974.
An attempt to gear classroom activity toward a thinking environment, using Piaget's theories. A bold curriculum is set forth, with more than 175 games described in detail, each with the intention of helping the child deal successfully with specific academic subjects.

Fugitt, Eva D. *"He Hit Me Back First!"* Rolling Hills Estate, CA: Jalmar Press.
An exciting book on self-esteem and problem solving, based on psychosynthesis. Focuses on empowerment and creativity of children. An excellent section on guided imagery.

Gilligan, Carol. *In a Different Voice*. Cambridge: Harvard University Press, 1982.
A significant book in the field of moral development. Focuses on the moral development of women.

Ginott, Haim. *Teacher and Child*. New York: Macmillan, 1972.
A human and practical book, helpful for establishing good communication and a moral climate of mutual respect between teacher and child.

Glasser, William. *Reality Therapy*. New York: Harper & Row, 1965.
Glasser makes two assumptions which we share, based on the need for self-love, self-esteem and appreciation and celebration of oneself. The first is that all emotional problems are symptomatic of the frustration of the fundamental human need for a sense of personal worth. Secondly, the self-image of the individual is the radical determining factor of all behavior.

Glasser, William. *Schools without Failure*. New York: Harper & Row, 1969.
Glasser examines the deficiencies in education that lead to school failure and emphasizes the structure of classroom meetings as a way of correcting the deficiencies. Presents three types of classroom meetings: (1) the social problem-solving meeting, (2) the educational diagnostic meeting, and (3) the open-ended meeting.

Gordon, Thomas. *Parent Effectiveness Training: The "No-Lose" Program for Raising Responsible Children*. New York: Wyden, 1970.

122

P.E.T. is an alternative to the authoritarian approach (children lose) and permissiveness (parents lose). It enables parents and teachers to show children how to solve their own problems without rancor, accusation, guilt or shame.

Gordon, Thomas. *P.E.T. in Action*. New York: Wyden, 1976.
An investigation of parents who have used P.E.T., with more information on active listening, "I" messages, and no-lose conflict resolution.

Gordon, Thomas and Peter H. *Teacher Effectiveness Training*. New York: Wyden, 1974.
Helpful to teachers in eliminating obstacles between themselves and students. "Obstacles" are defined as ways of phrasing messages that destroy further efforts at communication. "You're acting like a first grader, not someone ready for junior high." Moralizing and judgmental remarks make students feel that they are incompetent and irresponsible.

Gregson, Bob. *The Activity Truck Manual*. San Francisco: New Games Foundation, 1977.
A handbook of events, games and projects for creative playground programming, developed by Bob Gregson for the city of Hartford, CT. The activity truck was a mobile-arts unit equipped with simple materials and supplies that appeared on call to create "events" to foster group interaction, improved self-image and self-expression. The manual lists over twenty projects, including sidewalk drawing, shadow play, tire structure, big bubbles and new games. Well-illustrated and -explained, includes a bibliography and tips on sensitive playleading.

Haessly, Jacqueline. *Peacemaking: Family Activities for Justice and Peace*. 1980.
Order from 545 Island Road, Ramsey, NJ 07446. The author suggests ways for families to live together in peace and justice at home, with society and the world in general. Offers insight, information and activities from a Christian perspective.

Hafner, Helen. *Instant Guitar and Ukulele*. Arlington, VA: National Recreation and Park Association, 1974.
Teachers and others with no experience leading group singing (an important community-building exercise) may find that this skill can be quickly developed through the use of this manual. Geared to teaching without readings, notes and chords.

Haratonik, Peter, and Kit Laybourne. *Video and Kids*. New York: Gordon and Breach Science Publishers, 1974.
An excellent book on the concept of video and its history. Lots of good activities using video with kids.

Harrison, Marta, and the Nonviolence and Children Program. *For the Fun of It: Selected Cooperative Games for Children and Adults*. Philadelphia: Philadelphia Yearly Meeting.
Order from 1515 Cherry Street, Philadelphia, PA 19102. An excellent handbook on games that has been integrated into *A Manual on Nonviolence and Children*, edited by Stephanie Judson (see separate entry).

Hawley, R.C. *Values Exploration through Role Playing*. New York: Hart, 1979.
Provides step-by-step instruction for numerous formats for role-playing, one of the best ways to bring a class "alive" and to stimulate active involvement by all students.

Hendricks, Gay, and Russell Wills. *The Centering Book*. Englewood Cliffs, NJ: Prentice-Hall, 1975.
A series of activities that help children, parents and teachers to gain self-awareness through physical relaxation, movement, mind relaxation and centering (feeling one's inner strength). Also, includes sections on dreams and imagery.

Hendricks, Gay. *The Second Centering Book*. Englewood Cliffs, NJ: Prentice-Hall, 1977.
More awareness activities for parents, children and teachers.

Hennings, Dorothy Grant. *Smiles, Nods and Pauses*. New York: Citation Press, 1974.
A collection of verbal and nonverbal communication skills.

Hodgson, John, and Ernest Richards. *Improvisation*. London: Methuen, 1971.
Shows that drama can be a deeply influential community activity. The authors make many practical suggestions for situations and subjects upon which an improvisation may be built.

How to Turn War into Peace: A Child's Guide to Conflict Resolution. New York: Harcourt Brace Jovanovich, 1979.
A "Let Me Read" book for grades 3–6. An amusing demonstration of peacemaking and conflict resolution over sandcastles, including concepts and conflict resolution vocabulary.

Inside Out: A Guide for Teachers. National Instructional Television Center, 1973.
A handbook for teachers using the public television series, "Inside Out", designed for ages eight to ten. Material gathered from thirty-three educational broadcasting agencies, includes helpful material on conflict resolution. Now available in VHS format from video libraries.

Johnson, David W., and Roger T., Edye Holubec, and Roy and Pat Johnson. *Circles of Learning*.
Order from Interaction Book Co., 162 Windsor Lane, New Brighton, MN 55112. A brief introduction to cooperative learning by two of the pioneers and their associates. Provides procedure for implementing and supervising cooperative learning methods.

Johnson, David W., and Frank P. Johnson. *Joining Together: Group Theory and Group Skills*. 1982.
Order from Interaction Book Co., address above. An excellent book full of interesting experiential activities that focus on cooperative learning.

Johnson, David W. and Roger T. *Learning Together and Alone: Cooperation, Competition, and Individualization*.
Order from Interaction Book Co., address above. A manual for teachers that emphasizes basic principles of cooperative group learning and processes, and monitoring the development of social skills.

Johnson, David W. and Roger T., eds. *Structuring Cooperative Learning: Lesson Plans for Teachers*. 1984.
Order from Interaction Book Co., address above. Contains sample lesson plans for primary, intermediate and secondary grade levels.

Jones, John E., and J. William Pfeiffer. *Handbook of Structured Experiences for Human Relations Training*, vols. I–IV. Iowa City, IA: University Associates Press, 1970.
Full of excellent exercises in group processes that work well with adults and can be adapted for children.

Judson, Stephanie, ed. *A Manual on Nonviolence and Children*. Philadelphia: New Society, 1984.
One of the original books on conflict resolution and children, with emphasis on affirmation and parenting. An excellent companion to *Friendly Classroom*.

Katz, Neil H., and John W. Lawyer. *Communication and Conflict Management Skills*. 1983.
Order from Henneberry Hill Publishing Co., 2844 Henneberry Road, Pompey, New York 13138. Helpful theory and activities geared to older students and adults.

King, David. *Global Perspectives: A Humanistic Influence on the Curriculum*. 1975.
Order from the Center for Global Perspectives, 218 E. 18th Street, New York, NY 10003. This booklet offers curriculum on dealing with conflict, in two sections: K–3 and 4–6.

Kirschenbaum, Howard, and Sidney B. Simon. *Readings in Values Clarification*. Minneapolis, MN: Winston Press, 1973.
An excellent book on the theory and practice of values clarification. Sections include teaching school subjects with a focus on values.

Klagsbrun, Francine, ed. *Free to Be You and Me*. New York: McGraw-Hill, 1974.
A collection of songs, poems, pictures and stories concerning human liberation.

Klein, Alan. *Roleplaying*. New York: Association Press, 1956.
An overall view of roleplaying, particularly for improving meetings.

Kohlberg, L. *Collected Papers on Moral Development and Moral Education*. 1976.
Order from the Center for Moral Education, Larsen Hall, Harvard University, Cambridge MA. An excellent selection on the moral development of the child.

Kohn, Alfie. *No Contest: The Case Against Competition*. Boston: Houghton Mifflin, 1986.
A scholarly analysis, well documented, on how competition permeates the various aspects of our culture in counterproductive ways. Particularly impressive is the array of research demonstrating that intergroup and intragroup cooperative efforts produce better products as well as fostering more desirable interactions.

Kramer, Edith. *Art as Therapy with Children*. New York: Schocken Books, 1971.
Shows how art can be used as therapy and how the very act of creating becomes a powerful tool in the development of psychic organization. Author analyzes artwork in relation to problems children encounter such as aggression, sublimation and defense.

Kreidler, William J. *Creative Conflict Resolution: More than 200 Activities for Keeping Peace in the Classroom*. Glenview, Il: Scott, Foresman.
This excellent book not only provides a variety of structured procedures for dealing with conflict, but also exercises and activities for creating a classroom atmosphere in which conflict is less likely to occur. Students also come to understand their conflicts better and respond to them more creatively.

Lakey, Berit. *Meeting Facilitation: The No-Magic Method*. Philadelphia: New Society, 1975.
A compilation of theory, activities and diagrams based on the principles and experiences of nonviolent action, presented in a concise format.

Leonard, George. *The Ultimate Athlete*. New York: Viking, 1975.
By a redefinition of "games," Leonard suggests that increasing violence can be turned on itself and absorbed in the game. No defiance of the law, but a new context in which the law is part of the rules of the game.

Loesher, Elizabeth. *Conflict Management: A Curriculum for Peace, K–12* and *How to Avoid World War III at Home: Conflict Management for the Family*.
Order from the Conflict Center, 2564 So. Yates, Denver, CO 80219. Excellent resources to add to your curriculum materials.

Lowenfeld, Margaret. *Play in Childhood*. Portway Bath, GB: Cedric Chivers, 1969.

An analysis of the play activities of children: play as bodily activity, as repetition of experience, as demonstration of fantasy, etc. Attention is given to group games and children who cannot play.

McGinnis, Jim and Kathy, et al. *Educating for Peace and Justice: A Manual for Teachers*. 1981.
Order from the Institute for Peace and Justice, 4144 Lindell Boulevard, Room 400, St. Louis, MO 63108. Four volumes: *National Dimensions, Global Dimensions, Religious Dimensions*, and *Teacher Background Readings*. A thorough collection of current peace education literature from the first grade through college level. Of special relevance are "Conflict, Violence and Nonviolent Conflict Resolution" (in *National Dimensions*) and all of *Religious Dimensions*. Helpful bibliographies are included.

McGinnis, Jim and Kathy. *Parenting for Peace and Justice*. 1981.
Order from the Institute for Peace and Justice, address above. Part of the work of the Parenting for Peace and Justice Network. Includes family experiences and efforts to incorporate peace and justice into family life. A variety of activities from spiritual reflection to possible actions. The PPJ network is made up of parents and family life-leaders working to integrate family life and social concerns in a spirit of community, and has a strong Christian basis that is ecumenical in spirit.

Orlick, Terry. *The Cooperative Sports and Games Book: Challenge without Competition*. New York: Pantheon Books, 1978.
The idea behind this book is that people should play together, not against each other. It contains over one hundred games based on cooperation for every age, place and occasion.

Palmer, Pat. *Liking Myself*. San Luis Obispo, CA: Impact.
Helpful ideas on affirmation.

Palomares, Uvaldo. *A Curriculum on Conflict Management—Practical Methods for Helping Children Explore Creative Alternatives in Dealing with Conflict*. San Diego, CA: Human Development Training Institute, 1975.
A useful sourcebook on theory, lesson guides and game techniques for dealing with conflict resolution in the classroom.

Park, Mary Joan. *Creating a Peace Experience*. 1988.
Order from Little Friends for Peace, 4405 29th St., Mount Rainier, MD 20712. How to set up and run day camps following the approach of her *Peacemaking for Little Friends*, and including curriculum suggestions, activities, worksheets and cooperative games for ages four to ten.

Park, Mary Joan. *Peacemaking for Little Friends: Tips, Lessons and Resources for Parents and Teachers*. 1985.
Order from Little Friends for Peace, 4405 29th St., Mount Rainier, MD 20712. Practical suggestions on how to cultivate a nonviolent, problem-solving environment at home and in the neighborhood, peace activities for the classroom and at home, and peacemaking lessons for children four to twelve years old.

Patfoort, Pat. *An Introduction to Nonviolence: A Conceptual Framework*. 1987.
Order from the Fellowship of Reconciliation, Box 271, Nyack, NY 10960. Translated from the French by Priscilla Prutzman. Presents a theoretical view of nonviolence.

Peachey, J. Lorne. *How to Teach Peace to Children*. Scottdale, PA: Herald Press, 1981.
A useful resource for training children in nonviolence, produced by the New Call to Peacemaking, a coalition of the historic peace churches (Mennonites, Friends and Brethren).

Perr, Herb. *Making Art Together Step by Step*. San Jose, CA: Resource Publications, 1988.
Herb Perr's approach replaces trying to measure up to some authority's prescription for art and competition for rewards with methods to facilitate a student learning to find his or her way to contribute and interact while working on cooperative group projects which are grounded in the context of the child's environment, including her or his ethnic history. Twenty-four projects span elementary through secondary levels.

Piaget, J. *The Moral Judgment of the Child*. New York: Free Press, 1965.
Original French edition, 1932. The classic book on moral development.

Pietsch, W.V. *Human Be-ing: How to Have a Creative Relationship Instead of Power Struggle*. New York: New American Library.
An extremely perceptive, readable illustrated book. How to deal with the emotions behind conflict by listening, building trust, clarifying and risking changes in old patterns.

Pirtle, Sarah. *An Outbreak of Peace*. Philadelphia: New Society, 1987.
A novel about children who work toward creating a peaceful new society.

Prince, George M. *The Practice of Creativity*. New York: Collier Books, 1970.
This book discusses synectics, a structured method of problem solving. It explains why groups so often have problems getting things done. After defining the roles of a successful group meeting, Prince goes on to discuss ways of tapping everyone's creativity to find new solutions to problems.

Rainbow Activities: Fifty Multicultural/Human Relations Experiences. South El Monte, CA: Creative Teaching Press, 1977.

An activity book for human-relations skill building, specifically addressing the areas of cultural pluralism, self-image, feelings and values. Includes activities designed to help children appreciate their own and others' cultural heritage, and encourage stronger self-identity. The activities have been field-tested most successfully with students from grades K–8.

Renfield, Richard. *If Teachers Were Free*. New York: Dell, 1971.
Renfield holds that the basic defect in education is not the carrying out of the system, but the system itself. He proposes a new system based on the premise that children would learn far more if we responded to their curiosity. "We would be cooperating with nature rather than fighting."

Richmond, Arthur, ed. *Remo Bufano's Book of Puppetry*. New York: Macmillan, 1950.
Instructions for building a stage, puppets and marionettes, and producing plays. Four suggested plays included.

Rogers, Carl. *Freedom to Learn*. Columbus, Ohio: Charles E. Merrill, 1969.
The theme of the book is that students can learn and enjoy learning in an environment that encourages responsible participation in the selection and pursuit of goals.

Rosenberg, Marshall B. *A Model for Nonviolent Communication*. Philadelphia: New Society, 1983.
Understanding our feelings and learning to express them in ways that dissolve masks and open dialogue.

Satir, Virginia. *Peoplemaking*. Palo Alto, CA: Science and Behavior Books, 1972.
A valuable book for increasing the level and depth of relationships within the family and outside. The many experiments in communication make new insights come alive in practice.

Schniedewind, Nancy, and Ellen Davidson. *Cooperative Learning, Cooperative Lives*. Somerville, MA: Circle Books, 1987.
A sourcebook of learning activities for building a peaceful world. Contains over seventy-five activities in a variety of content areas.

Schniedewind, Nancy, and Ellen Davidson. *Open Minds to Equality: A Sourcebook of Learning Activities to Promote Race, Sex, Class and Age Equity*. Englewood Cliffs, NJ: Prentice-Hall.
This book offers a year-long curriculum of lesson plans and activities to help students become aware of and confront inequity, and to develop skills in working together.

Schrank, Jeffrey. *Teaching Human Beings: 101 Subversive Activities for the Classroom*. Boston: Beacon Press, 1972.
A good resource book with many ingenious group activities. Also includes an excellent bibliography.

Schwartz, Bill and Todd Pierson. *Finding Peace Within Ourselves: A One-Week Peace Unit for Elementary Schools*.
Order from Center for Peace Education, 1927 5th Street South, Minneapolis, MN 55454. Each page is designed as a lesson plan with many of the activities drawn directly from sources such as the CCRC handbook.

Shaftel, George and Fannie. *Roleplaying for Social Values*. Englewood Cliffs, NJ: Prentice-Hall, 1967.
What role should education play in moving a child from self-centeredness to concern for others? Through roleplaying, children can become aware of their own personal value system and be made sensitive to the feelings and welfare of others.

Simon, Sidney. *Values Clarification: A Handbook of Practical Strategies for Teachers and Students*. New York: Bantam, 1975.
A guide to exercises that help children to examine their own values.

Spolin, Viola. *Improvisation for the Theater*. Evanston, IL: Northwestern University Press, 1963.
A complete guide to theater exercises, with a special section for children.

Stanford, Barbara. *Peacemaking: A Guide to Conflict Resolution for Individuals, Groups and Nations*. New York: Bantam, 1975.
An early book on conflict resolution, focuses on high school.

United Nations Education. *Conflict and Conflict Resolution*.
Order from United Nations Education, 1351 Gilmore Avenue, Burnaby, BC CANADA V5C 4S8. These lessons explore the concept of conflict and peaceful, creative methods of conflict resolution. Starting with personal experiences of conflict in children's lives, the exercises expand to develop awareness of international conflict and violence.

Van Ornum, William, and Mary Wicker. *Talking to Children about Nuclear War*. New York: Continuum, 1984.
Practical, positive guidelines for parent/child discussions, based on research and hundreds of interviews, including actual dialogues. Written by a child psychologist and an educational journalist.

Weinstein, Matt and Joel Goodman. *Playfair: Everybody's Guide to Noncompetitive Play*. San Luis Obispo, CA: Impact Publishers, 1980.
A playful spirit runs throughout an effective rationale for cooperative games and the description of the activities. There are sections of the book for family games, mixers, energizers, leadership training, and learning games.

Weiss, Evelyn, Priscilla Prutzman, and Nancy Silber. *Children's Songs for a Friendly Planet*. Burnsville, NC: World Around Songs, 1986.
Order from CCRC, Box 271, Nyack, NY 10960. Full of songs from around the world for children K–6. Includes piano music and guitar chords.

Organizations

CCRC Branches and Related Programs

CCRC Branches

Children's Creative Response to Conflict
Box 271
Nyack, NY 10960
(914) 358-4601

The list of CCRC programs is constantly expanding. Also, addresses and contact people may change. Please write us for the most recent list. Information about CCRC facilitators and contacts in other countries is also available by writing to CCRC.

Other CCRC Programs in North America

Washington, DC
Marsha Blakeway, Coordinator
Box 7283   Arlington, VA   22207   (703) 532-5340

Santa Cruz, CA
CCRC
PO Box 624   Santa Cruz, CA   95061   (408) 426-3381

Canada
CCRC Canada, c/o Mary Anne Buchowski-Monnin
PO Box 7068   Station J.   Ottawa, Ontario K2A 3Z6 CANADA   (613) 224-2364

Tucson, AZ
CCRC, c/o Janice Ceridwen
AFSC   931 N. Fifth Avenue   Tucson, AZ 85705   (602) 623-9141

Phoenix, AZ
CCRC, c/o Dr. Ann Hardt
914 E. Laguna Drive   Tempe, AZ 85287   (602) 623-9141

Clarion, PA
CCRC, c/o John Smith
Clarion University   Department of Education
Clarion, PA 16214   (814) 226-2529

Troy, NY
CCRC Program, Interfaith Center for Peace with Justice/FOR
Box 1511   Troy, NY 12180   (518) 272-3920

Columbus, IN
CCRC, c/o Linda Emmert
Georgetown Road   Columbus, IN 47201   (812) 342-3990

Richmond, IN
CCRC, c/o Paul Barton-Kriese
417 Kinsey Street   Richmond, IN 47374   (317) 966-9286

Cincinnati, OH
CCRC, c/o Louise Gomer Bangel, Center for Peace Education
103 William Howard Taft Road   Cincinnati, OH 45219   (513) 221-4863 or 984-8847

Greenfield/Deerfield, MA
Judy Rubenstein
c/o Franklin Mediation Service
10 Osgood Street
Greenfield, MA   01301   (413) 774-7469

Peace Education Coordination
Traprock Peace Center
Woolman Hill, Keets Road
Deerfield, MA   01342   (413) 773-7427

Richmond, VA
Candace Powlick, Coordinator, Creative Conflict Resolution Team
14 N. Laurel Street   Richmond, VA   23220   (804) 358-1958

Seattle, WA
Students Creative Response to Conflict
2817 NW 61st Street   Seattle, WA   98107   (206) 789-6941

Apache Junction, AZ
CCRC, c/o Kietha Phyllis Gagnier
Adapting CCRC to Native American Issues
Box 4918   Apache Junction, AZ 85278   (602) 983-3108

Grand Rapids, MI
CCRC, c/o Andy Michaels-Weinburger
2243 Jefferson SE   Grand Rapids, MI 49507   (616) 245-2564
or contact Judi Buchman   (616) 454-1642

Related Programs

This list was prepared at the time of publication of the present edition. Addresses, telephone numbers and names of groups or contact people are subject to change. Individuals or groups are encouraged to send information to CCRC about such changes or about groups, programs or projects not listed which they deem valuable to include, so that this list may be expanded and updated. Users of this handbook may inquire about the availability of updated lists.

The notation *NL* in the description means that the group publishes a newsletter or periodical.

Aiki Works, Inc.
P.O. Box 7845   Aspen, Co 81612   (303) 925-7099
or P.O. Box 251   Victor, NY 14564   (716) 924-7302
Offers experiential workshops for adults and young people in conflict resolution, self-esteem, communication, leadership, and the Aiki Approach to Aikido.

Alternatives to Violence (ATV)
475 West Market Street   Akron, OH 44303   (216) 864-5442
Offers courses in peace and conflict resolution, mainly for Ohio secondary school teachers. Publishes *Alternatives to Violence* (see listing in bibliography under Bickmore, Kathy).

Alternatives to Violence Project (AVP)
15 Rutherford Place   New York, NY 10003   (212) 477-1067
Quaker-sponsored sister program to CCRC using similar themes and exercises. Workshops for prisoners and community groups, mainly in New York state but with growing national network (see description in chapter seventeen, page 80). NL

American Friends Service Committee (AFSC)
Peace Education Division   1501 Cherry Street   Philadelphia, PA 19102   (215) 241-7000
Quaker peace and international service organization with regional offices across the country, several of which support or sponsor CCRC programs. Active in human rights, civil rights and relief work. NL

Animal Town Game Company
PO Box 2002   Santa Barbara, CA 93120
Cooperative games for children and adults. Mail-order catalog.

Campfire, Inc. Resource Center
4601 Madison Avenue   Kansas City, MO 64112
Formerly Campfire Girls, has recently become co-ed. Peace education is one of its primary interests.

Community Boards Conflict Resolution Resources
Gail Sadalla
149 Ninth Street   San Francisco, CA 94103   (415) 552-1250
Offers workshops in mediation training for teachers and schools. NL

The Conflict Center
Elizabeth Loescher
2564 S. Yates   Denver, CO 80219   (303) 936-3286
Formerly Cornerstone. A peace organization with resources and training available on conflict resolution.

Consortium for Peace Research, Education, and Development (COPRED)
c/o Center for Conflict Resolution
George Mason University   4400 University Drive   Fairfax, VA 22030   (703) 323-2038
Devoted to networking, catalyzing and serving persons and institutions interested in scientific study, action, research and education on problems of peaceful social change and conflict resolution. NL

Council on Interracial Books for Children
1841 Broadway   New York, NY 10023
Resources to counter racism, sexism and other forms of bias in school and society.

Educators for Social Responsibility (ESR)
23 Garden Street   Cambridge, MA 02138   (617) 492-1764
National membership organization that focuses on nuclear-age education. Produces curriculum materials. NL

Educators for Social Responsibility (ESR/NY)
Tom Roderick
475 Riverside Drive, Room 939   New York, NY 10027   (212) 870-3318

The metropolitan New York branch of ESR, with whom CCRC in Nyack works closely. ESR and the New York City Board of Education sponsored a peace education program in the District 15 public schools. Publishes a draft teaching guide for K–6, "Resolving Conflict Creatively."

Equity Institute
PO Box 458   Amherst, MA 01002   (413) 256-6902
Offers workshops and resources dealing with name calling and homophobia. Focuses on grades 7–12. NL

End Violence Against the Next Generation (EVANG)
977 Keeler Avenue   Berkeley, CA 94708   (415) 527-0454
Seeks to eliminate corporal punishment from the schools. NL

Family Pastimes
RR 4   Perth, Ontario K7H 3C6   CANADA
Offers cooperative games and sports manuals. Mail-order catalog.

Fellowship of Reconciliation (FOR)
PO Box 271   Nyack, NY 10960   (914) 358-4601
An association of women and men who have joined together to explore the power of love and truth for resolving human conflict. Book distributor and publisher, seminars on nonviolence, many programs. Publishes *Fellowship* magazine. CCRC is an affiliate of FOR.

A Gentle Wind
Songs and Stories for Children
Box 3103   Albany, NY 12203
A distribution center for many audio tapes of children's music and storytelling. Mail-order catalog.

George Mason University
Center for Conflict Resolution
4400 University Drive   Fairfax, VA 22030   (703) 323-2038
Offers masters degree in conflict resolution.

Global Education Associates
Attn: Pat and Gerald Mische
475 Riverside Drive, Room 570   New York, NY 10115   (212) 870-3290
Network of persons in sixty countries concerned with world order, human rights, conflict resolution, etc. Publications, educational programs. NL

Global Learning
Jeffrey Brown
1018 Stuyvesant Avenue   Union, NJ 07083   (201) 783-7616
Workshops on global issues for schools, teachers and parents. Focus on conflict resolution, world hunger and international relations. NL

Global Perspectives in Education
218 E. 18th Street   New York, NY 10003   (212) 475-0850
Promotes education for democratic citizenship and cross-cultural perspectives. NL

Grace Contrino Abrams Peace Education Foundation
Fran Schmidt
Box 1153   Miami Beach, FL 33119   (305) 377-8161, extension 49
Produces excellent peace education and conflict resolution materials for grades K–12, including audio-visuals. NL

Green Circle Program, Inc.
1300 Spruce Street   Philadelphia, PA 19107
Has been working in schools for many years to encourage appreciation of racial and cultural differences.

Grindstone Co-op
PO Box 564, Station P   Toronto, Ontario   CANADA
Offers summer workshops on "raising children for a better world," on a beautiful Canadian island.

Hawaii School Mediation Alliance (HSMA)
Mel Ezer   College of Education   University of Hawaii at Manoa
West Hall Annex 2, Room 222   1776 University Avenue   Honolulu, HI 96822
Offers workshops and teacher training materials in mediation.

Humanitas International
Jim Wake, Assistant Director
PO Box 818   Menlo Park, CA 94026   (415) 324-9077
  Provides educational programs on human rights, disarmament and nonviolence. Has been very supportive of CCRC work. NL

Intercommunity Center for Justice and Peace
Kathleen Kanet
20 Washington Square North   New York, NY 10011   (212) 475-6677
  Offers peace and justice resources and workshops for educators. NL

Interhelp
PO Box 331   Northampton, MA 01061   (413) 586-6311
  A network of workshop facilitators on despair and empowerment, interpersonal relationships, and conflict resolution. NL

International Association for the Study of Cooperation in Education
Nancy and Ted Graves
136 Liberty Street   Santa Cruz, CA 95060   (408) 429-6550
  A networking membership organization focusing on cooperative learning. NL

International Peace Research Association (IPRA)
Chadwick Alger, Secretary General
199 W. 10th Avenue   Mershon Center, Ohio State University   Columbus, OH 43201
  Facilitates cooperation between scholars and educators throughout the world on peace and conflict resolution studies and research. NL

International Seminars on Training for Nonviolent Action
Beverly Woodward, Coordinator
Box 515   Waltham, MA 02254   (617) 891-0814
  Educates on nonviolent alternatives.

Jane Addams Peace Association
Ruth Chalmers, Executive Director
777 United Nations Plaza   New York, NY 10017   (212) 682-8830
  Helps to finance educational programs of the Women's International League for Peace and Freedom (WILPF). NL: *Building Peace*

Martin Luther King, Jr., Center for Social Change
449 Auburn Avenue, NE   Atlanta, GA 30312   (404) 524-1956
  Offers programs, seminars and training in nonviolence.

Milwaukee Peace Education Resource Center
Jacqueline Haessly, Director
2437 N. Grant Boulevard   Milwaukee, WI 53210   (414) 445-9736
  Produces materials on peacemaking, nonviolence and conflict resolution with special emphasis on children's and family-life activities. Facilitates parent and family workshops. NL: *Peacemaking for Children*

National Association for Mediation in Education (NAME)
Ann Gibson
425 Amity Street   Amherst, MA 01002   (413) 545-2462
  A networking organization for those working in school mediation programs.

National Catholic Educational Association
Rev. Msgr. John F. Meyers, President
1077 30th Street NW, Suite 100   Washington, DC 20007   (202) 293-5954
  Provides information on nonviolent conflict resolution and human rights.

National Peace Institute Foundation
Robert J. Conlon, Director
110 Maryland Avenue NE   Washington, DC 20002   (202) 546-9500
  Education and research on the U.S. Institute of Peace and similar institutions in other countries. Promotes nonviolent conflict resolution.

New York Board of Cooperative Educational Services (BOCES)
Conflict Resolution and Mediation Service
Barbara Brodsky
BOCES 2, Suffolk   8 43rd Street   Centereach, NY 11720   (516) 467-3610
  Offers training and curriculum materials in mediation for New York schools.

130

Nonviolence and Children Program (NVC)
Friends Peace Committee
1515 Cherry Street   Philadelphia, PA 19102   (215)241-7239
   Sister program to CCRC. Original publishers of *Manual on Nonviolence and Children*. Workshops for Quaker schools, parent groups and summer camps. Organizes parent support groups. NL

Parenting for Peace and Justice Network
Kathy and Jim McGinnis
Institute for Peace and Justice
4144 Lindell Boulevard, Room 400   St. Louis, MO 63108   (314) 533-4445
   An expanding network of parent support groups. Workshops and seminars are related to CCRC concepts. Publish books (see listings in bibliography under McGinnis) and audio-visuals.

Partners in Peacemaking
Naomi Drew
120 Finderne Avenue   Bridgewater, NJ 08807   (201) 231-1181
   School programs and workshops on cooperation, communication and conflict resolution in New Jersey. Publishes curriculum (see listing in bibliography under Drew, Naomi).

Peace Education Program
Betty Reardon
Box 171   Teacher's College   Columbia University   New York, NY 10027   (217) 678-3972
   Sponsors International Institute in Peace Education and intensive summer program in various universities around the world. Operates curriculum resource bank for teachers in metropolitan New York. Offers degree in peace education.

Pittenbrauch Press
Teddy Milne
15 Walnut Street   PO Box 553   Northampton, MA 01060
   Many peacemaking resources for children. Mail-order catalog, children's NL.

Project SMART (School Administrator's Alternative Resolution Team)
2 Lafayette Street   New York, NY 10007   (212) 577-7700
   A high school mediation project.

Resolution Center
Paul Wahrhaftig
7514 Kensington Street   Pittsburgh, PA 15221
   A conflict resolution organization. NL

Sagamore Conference Center
Sagamore Road   Racquette Lake, NY 13436   (315) 354-5311
   Offers workshops for teachers and others in the helping professions, in a beautiful Adirondack setting.

United States Institute of Peace
730 Jackson Place NW   Washington, DC 20503   (202) 789-5700
   Established by Congress in 1984 "to promote international peace and the resolution of conflicts." Offers grants to promote scholarship and education on peace and conflict resolution.

Wayne State University
Lillian Genser
Center for Peace and Conflict Studies   5229 Cass Avenue, Room 101   Detroit, MI 48202   (313) 577-3453/3468
   Offers peace education resources and resources for children.

Women's International League for Peace and Freedom (WILPF)
1213 Race Street   Philadelphia, PA 19107   (215) 563-7110
   Focus on disarmament, racism, peace education. NL: *Building Peace*.

World Council for Curriculum and Instruction (WCCI)
Dr. Maxine Dunfee, Executive Secretary
School of Education, Indiana University   Bloomington, IN 47405   (812) 335-4702
   Provides international programs on all aspects of curriculum and instruction, with a special emphasis on conflict resolution.

World without Weapons Project
4722 Baltimore Avenue   Philadelphia, PA 19143   (215) 724-1464 or 386-5129
   Workshops on imaging and inventing a world without weapons. An empowering experience for adults and children envisioning a weaponless world and how to achieve it. Encourages creative conflict resolution.

Index

Titles of games, exercises and songs are italicized. Page numbers of main descriptive entries are in bold.

Rainbows Not Radiation!
Bananas Not Bombs!
Grapes Not Guns!
Xylophones Not X-tinction!

WATERMELONS NOT WAR!
A SUPPORT BOOK FOR PARENTING
IN THE NUCLEAR AGE

by Kate Cloud, Ellie Deegan, Alice Evans,
    Hayat Imam, and Barbara Signer
Afterword by Dr. Helen Caldicott

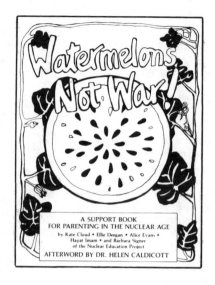

Five mothers in the Boston area have been meeting regularly for four years, to give each other support, to demystify nuclear technology—weapons and technology—into terms parents *and children* can understand, to find ways of acting which will give their children a future. The result is WATERMELONS NOT WAR! A SUPPORT BOOK FOR PARENTING IN THE NUCLEAR AGE.

—As written up in *Ms. Magazine, Whole Life Times, Sojourner*.

Large format. Beautifully illustrated.
Annotated Bibliography. 160 pages. 1984.
Hardcover: $24.95
Paperback: $9.95

A MANUAL ON NONVIOLENCE
AND CHILDREN
compiled and edited by Stephanie Judson
Foreword by Paula J. Paul,
    Educators for Social Responsibility
Includes "For the Fun of It! Selected Cooperative Games for Children and Adults"

Invaluable resource for creating an atmosphere in which children and adults can resolve problems and conflicts nonviolently. Especially useful for parents and teachers in instilling values today to create the peacemakers of tomorrow!

"Stephanie Judson's excellent manual has helped many parents and teachers with whom we have worked. An essential part of learning nonviolent ways of resolving conflicts is the creation of a trusting, affirming and cooperative environment in the home and classroom. This manual has a wealth of suggestions for creating such an environment. We highly recommend it."
—Jim and Kathy McGinnis
Parenting for Peace and Justice
St. Louis, Missouri

Large format. Illustrated.
160 pages. 1984
Hardcover: $24.95
Paperback: $12.95

To order, please add $3.00 to the price of the first copy and $1.00 for each additional copy (plus GST in Canada) for shipping. Send check or money order to New Society Publishers, P.O. Box 189, Gabriola Island, BC V0R 1X0, Canada.